Helion & Company Limited
Unit 8 Amherst Business Centre
Budbrooke Road
Warwick
CV34 5WE
England
Tel. 01926 499 619
Email: info@helion.co.uk
Website: www.helion.co.uk
Twitter: @helionbooks
https://helionbooks.wordpress.com/

Cover: Captain Leonard James Povey flying a Curtiss Hawk of the Cuban Army Air Corps over Havana in 1934. Povey was an American citizen hired by the-then Commander of the Cuban Army, General Fulgencio Batista, to train Cuban pilots. He was an iconic personality in the history of Cuban military aviation, famous for his acrobatic flights and for personally graduating 45 Cuban pilots. Povey decorated this aircraft with the Atuey aborigine on his own. (Artwork by Renato Dalmaso)

Designed and typeset by Mach 3 Solutions (www.mach3solutions.co.uk)
Cover design Paul Hewitt, Battlefield Design (www.battlefield-design.co.uk)

ISBN: 978-1-804517-17-8

British Library Cataloguing-in-Publication Data
A catalogue record for this book is available from the British Library

We always welcome receiving book proposals from prospective authors.

CONTENTS

Abbreviations and Acronyms 2
Acknowledgments 2
Introduction 2

1 The Genesis of Cuban Military Aviation 3
2 The Organisation and Evolution of the Cuban Army Aviation Corps 12
3 The CAEC in World War II and the Lend-Lease Program 23
4 Fulgencio Batista Zaldívar (1901-1973) 31
5 The Caribbean Legion in Cayo Confites 43
6 The Cuban Naval Air Force (FAN) 53
7 The CAEC in the late 1940s and early 1950s 66

Epilogue 73
Appendix 73
Endnotes 76
Sources 76
About the Authors 78

Note: In order to simplify the use of this book, all names, locations and geographic designations are as provided in *The Times World Atlas* or other traditionally accepted major sources of reference, as of the time of the described events.

ABBREVIATIONS AND ACRONYMS

AFB	Air Force Base
ANACRA	*Academia Nacional de Aviación Civil* (National Civil Aviation Academy)
ARP	American Republics Project (US)
ASR	Air Sea Rescue
CAEC	*Cuerpo de Aviación del Ejército de Cuba* (Cuban Army Aviation Corps)
CAP	Combat Air Patrol
FAERA	*Fuerza Aérea del Ejército de la Revolución Americana* (Air Force of the American Revolutionary Army)
FAC	Forward Air Controller
FAEC	*Fuerza Aérea del Ejército de Cuba* (Cuban Army Air Force)
FAN	*Fuerza Aérea Naval* (Naval Air Force)
FAR	*Fuerza Aérea Revolucionaria* (Revolutionary Air Force)
IFR	Instrument Flight Rules
MAP	Military Assistance Program (U.S.)
MDA	Mutual Defense Assistance (U.S.)
MDAP	Mutual Defense Assistance Program (U.S.)
MGR	*Marina de Guerra Revolucionaria* (Revolutionary Navy)
MMN	*Misión Militar Norteamericana* (North American Military Mission)
NCO	Non-Commissioned Officers
PAP	*Partido Acción Progresista* (Progressive Action Party)
PAU	*Partido Acción Unitaria* (Unitary Action Party)
PE	*Piloto de Enlace* (Liaison Pilot) (FAEC)
PC	*Piloto de Combate* (Combat Pilot) (FAEC)
PH	*Piloto de Helicóptero* (Helicopter Pilot) (FAEC)
PPC-O	*Partido del Pueblo Cubano (Ortodoxo)* (Cuban People's Party – Orthodox)
PRC-A	*Partido Revolucionario Cubano (Auténtico)* (Cuban Revolutionary Party – Authentic)
PSP	*Partido Socialista Popular (Partido Comunista)* (Popular Socialist Party – Communist Party)
RSMA	Reimbursable Military Aid (U.S.)
SME	*Servicio Militar de Emergencia* (Emergency Military Service)
USAAC	United States Army Air Corps
USAAF	United States Army Air Force
USAAS	United States Army Air Service
USAF	United States Air Force
VFR	Visual Flight Rules
W/O	Written Off

ACKNOWLEDGMENTS

The authors wish to express their deep gratitude to Tom Cooper for providing many of the pictures that illustrate this volume, which belong to the large Albert Grandolini collection, with some of the pictures coming from other private collections. Many of the photos in this volume have been obtained through different Facebook pages dedicated to Cuban military aviation.

INTRODUCTION

Cuba was the penultimate Spanish colony to achieve its independence, which occurred on 20 May 1902, so it could be said that it is a relatively young independent republic within the American continent. Spanish domination lasted several centuries until 1898, when the United States intervened in the war of independence, defeating the Spanish Army and occupying Cuba for three years.

Not many years passed in the independent life of Cuba before the beginning of aviation in the Caribbean country. The first aeronautical activities date back to 1910, and by 1913 the *Cuerpo de Aviación del Ejército de Cuba* (Cuban Army Aviation Corps, CAEC) had already been created, well before many other Latin American countries. In the years of World War I, Cuban military pilots trained in the United States were already very close to being sent to the Western Front in France, but the war ended before this could happen.

The CAEC grew over the years, and as Cuba supported the Allied cause in World War II, it benefited first from the Lend-Lease Program of the American government and then, in the post-war years, from other U.S. programmes such as the American Republics Program (ARP) and the Mutual Defence Assistance Program (MDAP), which improved not only the CAEC's aircraft supply but also the training of its pilots and mechanics.

This volume is divided into seven chapters that cover the genesis of Cuban military aviation, the organisation and evolution of the CAEC, Cuban military aviation in the Second World War, a short biography of a major protagonist of Cuban history, Fulgencio Batista, then the failed operation of the Caribbean Legion in Cayo Confites, the Cuban Naval Air Force (FAN) and finally the CAEC in the late 1940s and early 1950s before the creation of the Cuban Army Air Force (FAEC).

1

THE GENESIS OF CUBAN MILITARY AVIATION

Introduction

The first aeronautical demonstrations in Cuba occurred in the nineteenth century with a number of hot air balloon flights. The first flights were carried out by the French aeronaut Eugene Robertson on 19 March 1828 in Havana, while José Domingo Blinó became the first Cuban to rise in a hot air balloon on 30 May 1831. This balloon had been manufactured locally thanks to a popular subscription initiated by Captain General Dionisio Vives, with a demonstration taking place in the bullring of the Campo de Marte in Havana. The balloon crewed by Blinó ascended, and the winds carried it out of sight of the avid spectators. A tragic end at sea was immediately envisioned, but the winds subsequently took him to Pinar del Rio, where he finally descended in the midst of a heavy rain.

Much later, on 12 June 1856, the Portuguese-born Cuban resident Matías Pérez also ascended to the heights in a hot air balloon. Some months before, a number of flights had been carried out by another Frenchman, Eugene Godard. Pérez was Godard's assistant, and in fact he ascended with him at least three times. Then, excitedly, Pérez bought a hot air balloon for himself from Godard, which bore the name *Ville de Paris*. Pérez's first flight ascended from Campo de Marte in Havana and landed at Quinta Palatino, just outside the city. Unfortunately, the wind was strong on the day of his second flight, which had been scheduled for 28 June that same year, causing Pérez to delay his ascent. He finally decided to ascend at sunset around 7:00 p.m. The balloon rose rapidly with the warm air, possibly to more than 2,000 metres, and drifted north over the Florida Strait, never to be seen again. His tragic death earned him a place both in Cuban aviation history and in popular culture. His disappearance coined the popular century-old phrase '*Voló como Matías Pérez*' (flew away like Matías Pérez), used when referring to a missing person or object.

The first attempt to create military aviation in Cuba dates back to the early 1890s. An agronomic engineer named Arturo Comas Pons, after reading the principles formulated in 1809 by the English engineer Sir George Cayley, designed a small-scale monoplane that weighed 28 ounces. The frame was made of wooden rods and paper, the propeller blades were made of cedar, and the engine was a reinforced clock machine. This scale model managed to fly up to the height of the roof of a house. Once the principle was proven, his full-scale 'aerial velocipede', as it was called, would be built with steel, aluminium and canvas and run on pedal propulsion, although Comas himself admitted that muscular force would be insufficient

Examples of various aeronautical demonstrations in Cuba in the nineteenth century: The Frenchman Eugene Robertson was the first to ascend in a balloon in 1828 (top left). The first Cuban balloonist was José Domingo Blinó, who flew in a balloon in 1831 (bottom left). The Portuguese national in Cuba Matías Pérez (left) in the basket of the *Ville de Paris* balloon with the French aeronaut Eugene Godard (right) (top right) in 1856. One of the flights made in the *Ville de Paris* balloon with Godard and Pérez on board (bottom right). (Open source)

and thought of using an electrical engine instead. As with the model, the propeller would be made of cedar.

In 1893, Comas wrote a letter to José Martí, patriot and hero of Cuban Independence, regarding his flying machine and the possibility of using it in the war that would surely occur to free Cuba from the Spanish yoke. Comas suggested in his letter that half a dozen such velocipedes could drop bombs on the enemy at nighttime, creating panic among the soldiers. Obviously the intention of using an aerial machine in war was a very advanced idea for 1893, and Martí did not pay attention to such a request, especially because the meagre revolutionary resources available were being used to buy rifles and ammunition. Comas then travelled to the United States,

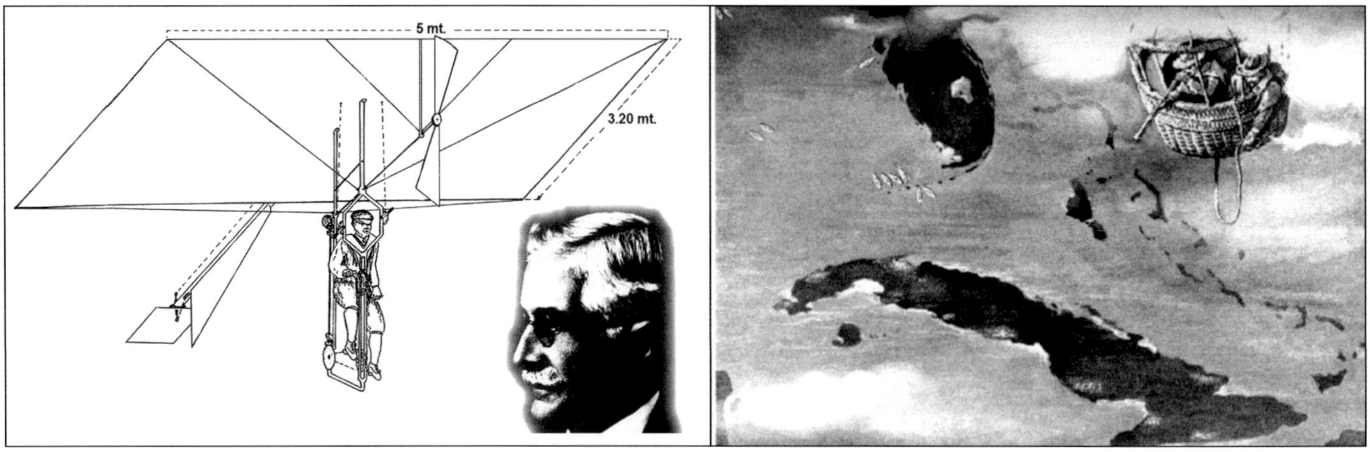

Unrealised plan for a velocipede, designed by the Cuban inventor and agronomic engineer Arturo Comas Pons (left). An allegory of the aerial observations made by American troops in a hot air balloon during the Spanish-Cuban-American War of 1898 (right). (ecured.cu)

Scenes from the Cuban War of Independence: the hero and martyr of the struggle, the Cuban José Martí (top left), rebel Cuban troops (top right), U.S. Army troops (bottom left) and Spanish troops (bottom right). (Albert Grandolini collection via Tom Cooper)

Cuban-American Aída de Acosta Root Breckinridge (left) became the first woman in the world to fly solo. She did it on the airship 'No. 9' (centre) belonging to the Brazilian aviation pioneer Alberto Santos-Dumont (right) in Paris, France, on 27 June 1903. (Open source)

where he tried to convince the U.S. Army of his ideas, but the project was considered unviable.

Although the U.S. Army had a balloon corps briefly during the Civil War, it did not conduct ballooning operations again until 1892, when it established a balloon section within the army signal corps. Nevertheless, when war with Spain broke out in 1898, the army's 'air arm' consisted of a single hand-sewn balloon. Despite incredible difficulties, Lieutenant Colonel Joseph Maxfield of the balloon section succeeded in getting the balloon to Cuba. The U.S. Army's first balloon flight in Cuba was carried out successfully on 30 June 1898, with Maxfield and Sergeant Ivy Baldwin on board. Pleased with the results, Maxfield took Lieutenant Colonel George M. Derby aloft for the second flight. He then assigned Lieutenant W. S. Volkmar to make a third ascent with a Cuban general named Castillo. The flights confirmed the presence of the Spanish fleet in Manila harbour.

Enthusiastically positive reports were thereupon made to U.S. expedition commander, General William R. Shafter. Even more impressive were the observations made on 1 July, during the critical Battle of San Juan Hill. An initial captive ascent was made at some distance from the battle, after which Lieutenant Colonel Derby ordered the balloon moved to within 650 yards of the Spanish trenches. From this position, the balloon observers were able to discover a trail that relieved congestion and enabled the troops to advance rapidly. It also allowed the American and Cuban forces to deploy two columns against the Spanish, one along the main road and another along the trail. The observers also proved effective in directing and redirecting artillery fire. Indeed, some historians believe that the use of the balloon was a determining factor in the American victory.

That valuable information came at a high cost, however. The balloon, badly damaged by enemy fire, was rendered beyond repair. In fact, the Spanish commanders claimed they had it shot down! The only crew member on its final flight was Sergeant Balwin, but he was unharmed. Now convinced of the value of balloon observation, the army organised a second balloon company, equipped with two balloons, but it was not ready before the war ended. Despite the success of balloon reconnaissance in the Spanish-American War, however, the U.S. Army disbanded the balloon detachment in 1899.

Meanwhile, still at the dawn of the twentieth century, the Cuban American Aída de Acosta Root Breckinridge made a solo flight aboard the Santos Dumont airship 'No. 9' on the outskirts of Paris on 9 June 1903, becoming the first Latin American woman to fly in the history of aviation.

The birth of the Cuban Army Aviation Corps (CAEC)

It was on 7 May 1910 that an aircraft was flown for the first time in Cuba. It was a Voisin biplane equipped with a 50-hp Buchet engine that belonged to 27-year-old French pilot André Bellot. The Voisin took off from the Almendares horse tracks, reaching a height between 25 and 30 metres. When the pilot tried to change course due to strong winds, parts of the aircraft detached, and the Voisin crashed shortly after, with no consequences for the pilot. Bellot flew around two and a half minutes and a distance of approximately 3 kilometres from the horse tracks, with an average speed of 70 kph. Havana thus became the third Latin American city to see the flight of an aircraft, after Mexico City and Buenos Aires.

On 30 January 1911, a 25-year-old Canadian pilot, John Alexander Douglas McCurdy, attempted to fly from Key West in the United States to Havana in Cuba in a Curtiss biplane but fell into the sea and was rescued by a U.S. Navy destroyer. The biplane was also rescued and repaired. The same pilot later made a successful flight from Camp Columbia to Farola del Morro in his Curtiss equipped with a 60-hp Belmont engine on 5 February 1911.

A few days before this, the first air shows had been held at Camp Columbia, near Havana, led by the American pilots James Ward, Lincoln Beachy, Gardiner Hubbard and George F. Russell from the Curtiss Aviation School, before an immense audience, given the novelty of these types of shows. Other foreign pilots performed in several aviation events organised in Cuba in those years, such as Roland Garros, René Barrier, René Simón, John Frisbie, Alfred Moisant, and Saint Croix Johnstone, among others. Some exhibition flights were also carried out in several other cities in Cuba, such as Colón, Cienfuegos, Santa Clara, Guantánamo, Santiago de Cuba, Manzanillo, Matanzas, San Antonio de los Baños and Cárdenas.

It would not be until 2 January 1912, however, that Havana would see the first flight by a Cuban pilot, when Agustín Parlá Orduña, accompanied by the American pilot Charles F. Walsh, flew in a Curtiss hydroplane. A few months later, on 20 April, Parlá, born in Key West, Florida, on 10 October 1887, the son of Cuban immigrants, graduated as a pilot from the Curtiss Aviation School in Miami and thus became the first accredited Cuban aviator.

The first aircraft flown in Cuba was a Voisin biplane piloted by the Frenchman André Bellot (left) in 1910. (Open source) Also in 1910, the Canadian pilot John Alexander Douglas McCurdy (right) attempted to fly between Key West and Havana in a Curtiss biplane but fell into the sea, being rescued by a U.S. Navy destroyer. (City of Toronto Archives)

Agustin Parlá (centre with white shirt and tie), the Father of Cuban Aviation, in Miami Beach, 1912, at the Curtiss Aviation School where he learned to fly. (Open source)

Agustin Parlá (third from the right with hat and tie), posing with his Morane-Saulnier G and several civilians and soldiers in Cuba in 1913. (Open source)

Captain Domingo Rosillo del Toro posing with the Morane-Saulnier G with which he flew from Key West to Havana on 17 May 1913 (left) and wearing a Cuban Army uniform with all his decorations (right). (Historia de la Aviación Militar Cubana)

On 22 October of that same year, Domingo Rosillo del Toro, who was born in Oran, Algeria, on 8 October 1878 but became a Cuban citizen later, received his pilot's license from the International Aeronautical Federation at the *Aero Club de France* in Paris. He made his first flight in Cuba on 13 March 1913, over Havana's Camp Columbia in his Morane-Saulnier G with a 50-hp Gnome engine. Three days later, he performed his second flight in public over the city of Havana. On 11 April of that year, Rosillo broke the height record held by the French aviator Roland Garros by 227 metres, reaching an altitude of 2,300 metres. Then on 17 May, Rosillo carried out the first international flight in Latin American aviation, establishing a world distance record by flying the 90 miles from Key West to Havana in his Morane Saulnier G monoplane in 2 hours and 40 minutes, landing at Camp Columbia. As a result, he won a $10,000 prize for his achievement and was granted not only Cuban citizenship but also the rank of captain in the Cuban Armed Forces. Just two days after Rosillo's epic flight, pilot Agustín Parlá Orduña also successfully crossed the Florida Strait in a float-equipped Curtiss pusher aircraft, landing in Mariel Bay in northern Cuba. He had flown exactly 117 miles at an average speed of 64 miles per hour.

On 5 July 1913, the so-called *Cuerpo de Aviación del Ejército de Cuba* (Cuban Army Aviation Corps, CAEC), equipped with a Curtiss model FS flying boat purchased that spring, was created as an auxiliary arm of the Cuban Army. In so doing, Agustín Parlá, considered the father of Cuban aviation, was granted the rank of captain and appointed chief flying instructor of the CAEC in August.

The first two aircraft of the CAEC: a Curtiss FS flying boat (left) (City of Toronto Archives) and a Morane-Saulnier G (right). (History of Cuban Military Aviation)

However, the corresponding decree still recognised Parlá as merely a civilian employee of the army, and it would only be years later that he would be officially designated a reserve captain.

A third early Cuban aviator was Jaime González Crocier, who was born in Cienfuegos on 13 February 1895. Crozier began flying in his native Cuba on 23 February 1914, and in May of that same year, emulating the feats of the previous two pilots mentioned, he made a 285-kilometre flight from Cienfuegos to Havana aboard his Morane-Saulnier G. The pilot Rosillo del Toro had made a similar 147-kilometre flight between Pinar del Río and Havana on 25 February of that same year, and in December, a Spanish aviator, José Piñeiro, made the first full looping of Cuba.

On 13 October 1915, Jaime González Crocier was named honorary captain, and his Morane-Saulnier G aircraft, which had once belonged to Agustín Parlá, was acquired for the CAEC. That same year, General José Martí (son of José Julián Martí Pérez, the hero of Cuban Independence), commander of the Cuban Army, sent Captain Parlá to the Curtiss factory in Buffalo, New York, to be trained in seaplanes for the purpose of establishing a military aviation school for Cuban officers. On 24 September 1916, Parlá flew successfully over Niagara Falls while in Buffalo and won an international competition.

On 11 February 1917, the so-called La Chambelona Rebellion took place. The liberals took up arms in protest against the electoral fraud that favoured President Mario García Menocal. The rebels were led by General Gómez, who came to dominate virtually all of the provinces of Camagüey and Oriente, as well as part of Las Villas. During this uprising, Captain Jaime González Crocier dropped pamphlets from an aircraft to the rebels, urging them to surrender and threatening them with aerial actions, this being the first military

Another pioneering Cuban aviator, Captain Jaime González Crocier (above) and his Morane Saulnier G acquired by the CEAC (below). (CubaMuseo.com Project)

action carried out by Cuban military aviation. A month into the campaign, General Gómez was taken prisoner along with others of his followers, many of whom were executed while others were granted political amnesty.

General Mario García Menocal (1913-1921), under whose presidency the Cuban Army Aviation Corps was created. (Open source)

The First World War

In April 1917, the United States declared war on the European Central Powers during World War I. Cuba did the same and President General Mario García Menocal proposed sending troops to the European front, which the American government opposed, but a compromise was reached to send a squadron of Cuban pilots. The proposal on the part of Colonel Manuel María Coronado, a member of the Cuban Senate, then arose to send a group of 33 officers and non-commissioned officers of the Cuban Army, under the command of Captain Francisco Terry Sánchez, to train as military pilots in the United States. The officers were sent to the University of Texas at Austin for pilot training and the non-commissioned officers to Kelly Field in San Antonio to become aviation mechanics. All of them would be part of the Cuban Air Squadron to fight in Europe on the Western Front in the service of the French Army. Many of the pilots had previously been university students in France, so they already spoke French.

On 14 September 1917, the so-called *Le Escuadrille Cubaine* (The Cuban Squadron) was created to fight in France. The squadron was organised by Lieutenant Santiago García-Díaz Campuzano, who would receive the Medal of Valour from the French Army during the war. In order to equip the aforementioned squadron, the Cuban government placed an order for 20 combat aircraft in the United States, although the type of aircraft was not disclosed.

On 15 May 1918, a new law passed by the Cuban government authorised the creation of an aviation school. A few days later, President Menocal signed decree No. 1181, creating the Army Aviation Corps and the Military Aviation School. In August of that year, Captain Francisco Terry, who had fought in Europe as a member of the United States Lafayette Squadron, was appointed commander of the *Escuadrón de Combate No. 1* (First Combat Squadron), comprising 10 pilots and 20 aviation mechanics, while Lieutenant Santiago Campuzano would be in charge of the *Escuadrón de Combate No. 2* (Second Combat Squadron). On 6 September 1918, the 30 members of the First Squadron arrived at Kelly Field in San Antonio, home of the 322nd Squadron of U.S. Army Aviation, for training. The First World War ended before the Cuban Squadron could continue its training and embark for Europe, however. The squadron eventually returned home to Cuba in April 1919.

Despite this, several Cuban pilots served in the French *Aéronautique Militaire* during the First World War through the aegis of the French Foreign Legion. They included:

- Francisco 'Panchito' Terry Sánchez. Sánchez was awarded the French Croix de Guerre with a Palm Leaf, the Russian Cross of Saint George and the Military Cross of Romania for his military service. He flew in Nieuport 11 fighters during the war.
- Santiago García Díaz-Campuzano. Díaz-Campuzano's most notable military achievement was a nighttime bombing carried out 46 km deep inside the German lines that lasted four and a half hours during a terrible snowstorm on a night in February 1915. He was wounded twice in combat against enemy aircraft and then joined the Paris Defence Squadron, where he remained until the end of the war.
- Rogelio Bablab. Bablab was killed during a dogfight with a German plane on 21 May 1918. He was awarded the French Military Cross in 1915 for bravery.
- J. B. Briol. Briol was cited twice in the Order of the Day of his regiment, twice in that of his division, and in that of the aviation corps, in recognition of his heroic services.

- Juan Sánchez. A pilot in the service of France and son of the French army medical captain Juan Sánchez Toledo, Sánchez died in combat when he was shot down by a German biplane.
- Florencio Paldal. Paldal travelled to France in 1914 to become a military pilot and served as a volunteer in the French *Aéronautique Militaire* during World War I.

The following Cuban aviators also served in the British Royal Flying Corps (RFC):

- Jack Lethbridge del Monte. Del Monte fought in the British RFC with the rank of second lieutenant aviator.
- Oscar B. Santamaría Lainé. After graduating as a pilot in the Canadian Air Force with the rank of second lieutenant, Lainé attended the advanced flight course in England. He was stationed with the 216th Night Bombing Squadron of the Royal Flying Corps in France until the end of the war. He remained as part of the occupation army, being the first pilot to fly mail between Marquise, France, and Cologne, Germany. Discharged from the Canadian Army as a first lieutenant, Lainé went to the United States in 1919 and worked in the American airmail service for six months flying De Havilland DH-4B aircraft.

Finally, there was a Cuban pilot who served in the U.S. Naval Aviation named Max J. Baehr, who held the rank of lieutenant. The scion of a distinguished family from Cienfuegos, Baehr was residing in the United States studying for a career at a university when the U.S. declared war against Germany. He entered military service and was sent to fight in Europe. He was demobilised in 1919.

The postwar years and the acquisition of aircraft

The first U.S. Army air mission arrived in Cuba immediately after the war. It was led by Captain C. Charbourne and Lieutenant D. G. Richardson, with a Lieutenant Kelly joining later. Nine Curtiss JN-4D Jenny biplanes had been purchased in December 1918 for the Cuban Military Aviation School, but only six of them had arrived by this time, the other three having been badly damaged en route. The base was established at Camp Columbia in Havana. One of the Jennys was conferred with the name Sunshine by Georgina Menocal, daughter of President Menocal. It was in this biplane that Captain Parlá would make a flight to the United States from Havana, and it would also be with this aircraft that the first aerial photos of the Cuban capital were taken.

The first official flight with the Jennies took place on 11 May 1919, when Captain Francisco Terry flew over Havana's Malecón

Three CAEC Curtiss JN-4D Jennies, the one in the foreground bearing serial number 4, in 1920. (Historia de la Aviación Militar Cubana, HAMC)

Captain Jaime González Crocier posing with a Bleriot XI. (Vintage Cuba)

esplanade. On that same day, the Camp Columbia military base was inaugurated as an airfield by President Menocal and leading members of his government.

As with every beginning in aviation, there were some accidents. On 7 July 1919, a Jenny crewed by Sgt Santiago Alemán and Sgt José Díaz crashed while performing a loop at too low an altitude at Camp Columbia; both pilots were killed. On 4 July 1920, a Morane-Saulnier G crewed by Lt Jaime González Crocier crashed in the Luyanó neighbourhood near Havana during takeoff, costing him his life. On a more positive note, the first cross-country flight was carried out by three CAEC Jennies from Havana to Saguá la Grande, over 200 kilometres to the east, with a stop in Jovellanos on 10 October of that year. Due to the accidents mentioned above, the CAEC requested the purchase of six Curtiss JN-6H trainers from the U.S. Army Air Service, but this acquisition did not come to fruition, at least on that occasion.

On 7 March 1920, the first night flight in Cuba was carried out when the American aviator Fred W. Kelly, accompanied by Agustín Parlá, flew over the city of Havana in an entirely red Curtiss JN-4D Jenny dubbed *Diablo Rojo* (Red Devil). The aircraft performed a series of acrobatic manoeuvres, including loops, before a stunned audience while Parlá launched firecrackers that exploded in multiple colours, creating a unique spectacle. Parlá subsequently resigned from the army and, in 1928, emigrated to the United States, where he worked as a flight instructor at an aviation school in Cincinnati, Ohio. He would return to Cuba in 1935, where he was appointed General Inspector of Airports. His life would end tragically on 31 July 1946. A certain sector of the press had proclaimed Rosillo as the true pioneer of aviation in Cuba and not Parlá, while various detractors in the government made his life impossible. Unable to bear the strain any longer, he committed suicide with a high dose of barbiturates.

In 1921, two Cuban Army officers were selected to receive flight training in the U.S. Army Air Service: Captain M. Arozarena at March Field in California and 2nd Lt Eddie Laborde at Carlstrom Field in Florida, while two others attended the Observation School at Fort Sill in Oklahoma and the Air Service Pilots School in Arcadia, Florida, respectively. By May 1923, the CAEC, having expanded its facilities at Camp Columbia, had a staff of 18 officers and 97 enlisted men. Its list of competencies also increased when Lieutenant Guillermo Martull performed the first successful free parachute jump on 4 July 1925.

In 1924, the CAEC received nine Vought QO-2 Corsair fighters. These fighters still had the vertical red-white-blue stripes on their rudders. (Vought Aircraft Industries/Albert Grandolini Archives via Tom Cooper)

Three CAEC Vought QO-2 Corsairs parked at Camp Columbia near Havana in the mid-1920s. (Historia de la Aviación Militar Cubana, HAMC)

These photos, although of poor quality, show two De Havilland DH-4M-1 bombers belonging to the CAEC in the 1920s. On the left, a DH-4 is parked next to a QO-2 Corsair at Camp Columbia, while on the right, a DH-4 is being prepared for a routine flight. Both aircraft still have the original red-white-blue vertical stripes on their rudders, which would be replaced later by the colours of the Cuban flag. (from the video *Tiempos Heroicos de la Aviación Cubana*)

In 1924, the Cuban government ordered the purchase of four (later increased to nine) Vought QO-2 Corsair multipurpose fighter biplanes with interchangeable landing gear with floats. Towards the end of that year, the purchase of ten D.H.4 biplanes and two Curtiss JN-6 biplanes was also ordered, as well as 10 spare Liberty engines. On 11 February of that year, a JN-4D flown by Lt Alberto Valdes González crashed at Camp Columbia, resulting in the latter's death.

The conspiracy of Veterans and Patriots

In 1923 and 1924, a political group called *Movimiento Nacional de Veteranos y Patriotas* (Veterans and Patriots National Movement) planned to acquire six Curtiss JN-4D Jenny biplanes for the purpose of bombing military installations belonging to the government of President Alfredo Zayas y Alfonso. The intended rebel pilots, Rubén Martínez Villena, José Antonio Fernández de Castro and Calixto García Martínez-Ibor, were undergoing training in Ocala, Florida, but were betrayed and arrested, thus rendering the movement stillborn before it could carry out its operations against the government. Other rebel leaders were bribed by the government, and thus the movement was stamped out. It is known that the Zayas government had also hired the services of the French aviators Charles Nungesser, Andre Bellot and Maurice Weiss to counter any action by the plotters, which was ultimately unnecessary.

2

THE ORGANISATION AND EVOLUTION OF THE CUBAN ARMY AVIATION CORPS

On 20 May 1925, General Gerardo Machado Morales assumed the presidency of Cuba. A few days later, the new president ordered the reorganisation of the CAEC, appointing Captain Mario Torres Menier for this purpose. Three new hangars were then built, and the headquarters building, aviation mechanics workshops and the parachute department were expanded. It was during General Machado's administration that Cuban military aviation underwent significant growth.

At that time, the pilot cadre consisted of Captains Gustavo Alfonso, Pablo Alonso, Arístides Agüero, Miguel de Jesús Bannatyne, José Barrientos, Javier Bazán, Jorge Cao, Miguel Ángel González, Eduardo Laborde Moliner and Lieutenants Ciro Leonard, Rogelio Morlotte Caballero, Guillermo Martull, Alberto Ponce de León Hernández, José Terry Jiménez, Carlos Torres de Navarra, Alberto Valdés González, Manuel Vidal Lazaga and Guillermo González Vizcay. In 1925, the CAEC still comprised only 119 servicemen, including 18 officers (nine captains, five first lieutenants and four second lieutenants), 26 NCOs (15 sergeants and 11 corporals) and 75 troops, and possessed a grand total of 24 aircraft of all types.

In 1926, two CAEC Vought Corsairs, crewed by Captain Eduardo Laborde and Lieutenant Guillermo Martull, carried out Cuban military aviation's first international flight, flying from Havana to Camagüey and then to Port-au-Prince in Haiti. That same year, in October, a hurricane severely damaged the CAEC facilities and aircraft at Camp Columbia, so practically everything had to be rebuilt under the leadership of Major Ovidio Ortega y Campos. Luckily, all the damaged planes were repairable, although spare parts had to be acquired. In November of that year, six sets of wings, rudders, stabilisers and vertical fins were purchased to repair the DH-4s.

1926 also saw a major reorganisation of the Cuban Army. According to the new law, the army consisted of a general staff; infantry, artillery and cavalry branches; an aviation corps; signals and engineering; audit and veterinary services; military schools; a rural guard; and a militia. The number of officers, NCOs and rank-and-file troops at that time comprised 13,000 effectives.

In 1927, another American military mission, this time headed by then-Captain Rosenham Beam and composed of pilots Lieutenants Jack Hadgson and James Gillespie and two mechanics, Master Sergeants Joseph Biando and Conrad O'Bryan, arrived in Cuba at the request of President Machado to reorganise the CAEC. One of the first actions of this mission was to decommission and retire all the Jenny biplanes, as they were now old and unsafe, leaving the active air fleet comprised of the Vought Corsairs and the Boeing-built De Havilland DH-4M-1s. In addition, the purchase of four, later

Five Vought QO-2 Corsair fighters of the CAEC at Alacranes airport with an American-registered civilian plane, a Curtiss Robin C-1, on 3 August 1930. (History of Cuban Military Aviation, HAMC)

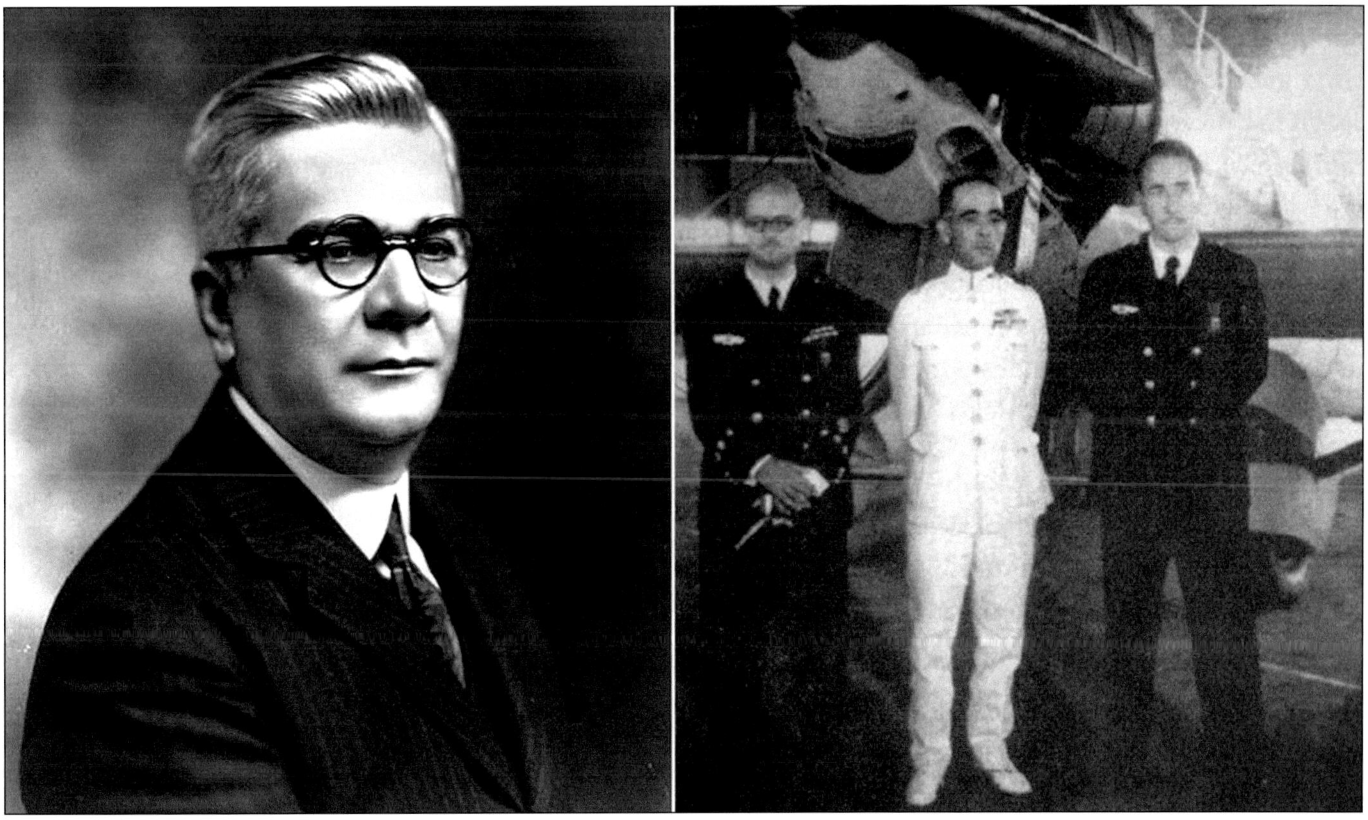

Cuban president General Gerardo Machado Morales (1925-1933) (left) (Open Source). Captain Mario Torres Menier posing between the Spanish aviators Barberán and Collar in front of their Breguet 19 Super Bidón in Havana in 1933 (right). (Cuba Militar.org)

Various images from a Cuban documentary from the early 1930s showing CAEC Vought O2U-1A and O2U-3A Corsair fighters on training flights over Havana. (stills from the video *Tiempos Heroicos de la Aviación Cubana*)

A CAEC Consolidated PT-3 Husky primary trainer still at the factory in the U.S. in 1928 before its delivery to Cuba. (General Dynamics Corporation)

increased to ten, Consolidated PT-3 Huskies for primary training was ordered, which arrived in Cuba in the first months of 1928. That same year, on 17 April, one of the PT-3s, crewed by Lt Alberto Ponce de León Hernández as flight instructor and student pilot Frigate Ensign Raúl Pérez Terrada, took off from Camp Columbia for a routine training flight never to return. It was feared that they crashed into the ocean and their remains were never found.

More combat aircraft were ordered in 1929, including five Curtiss P-6S Hawk fighters, six Vought O2U-1A Corsairs and eight Vought O2U-3A Corsairs. Additional Corsairs were ordered in the ensuing years, with the total eventually reaching 26 aircraft of this type. In January 1932, four Curtiss Hawk I fighters, one Aeronca C-3, two Waco 9s and two Waco 10s were also acquired, with the Wacos being a donation from the *El País* newspaper.

Five Curtiss P-6S fighters were acquired for the CAEC in 1929. (Curtiss-Wright)

Two CAEC Curtiss 35 Hawk I fighters with serial numbers 20 and 21. Captain Leo Povey is posing with Hawk serial number 21, which became his personal aircraft during his four-year stay in Cuba as the head of the Military Aviation School. (P.R.B.J. Collection)

The only Aeronca C-3 that was in service in the CAEC. (History of Cuban Military Aviation, HAMC)

Pilots and aerial gunners pose in front of an impressive flight line of CAEC Vought O2U Corsairs at Camp Columbia in the late 1920s. (Vintage Cuba)

Regarding the Aeronca C-3 (serial number unknown), it would be flown by Captain Eduardo Laborde on a long-haul flight from Havana to Guatemala City to Mexico City and back again, a distance of 2,737 miles, between 20 April and 29 July 1932 – an impressive feat considering the type of aircraft used.

The Military Aviation School

President Machado reopened the Military Aviation School on 5 March 1928, which had been rebuilt after the impact of the hurricane on Camp Columbia. The new facilities had large classrooms, laboratories, offices and barracks for 25 cadets. The teaching staff consisted of Lieutenant Colonel Antonio Mesa y Valdés; Medical Captain Armando de la Torre; flight instructors Captains Mario Torres Menier, Armando Castellán Villageliú, Eduardo Laborde Moliner and Guillermo Martull; first lieutenants Agustín Rodríguez, Demetrio Ravelo Hernández, José A. Terry Jiménez, James Gillespie and Pablo A. Rosado Rodríguez; second lieutenants Rogelio Morlotte, Faustino López Neira and Florindo Fernández Prieto; and Naval Ensign Oscar Rivery.

The curricular training of aviation cadets included subjects such as military courtesy, hygiene and military administration, army regulations, service etiquette, infantry and guard service, criminal and prosecutorial law, maintenance of aerial material, aerodynamics, parachutes, telegraphy, aviation instruments, international air regulations, engines and systems, aircraft alignment, maps, air navigation, pursuit, attack, air tactics, meteorology, air weapons, sights and synchronisation of machine guns, bombing, bombing sights, bombs and explosives, communications and signals, aerial photography and aerial observation.

The prestige of the CAEC under the administration of the U.S. mission led by Beam spread to other countries like the Dominican Republic, Panama and even Ecuador, and they began sending cadets with scholarships to be trained as military pilots in 1930 and 1931. By February 1931, the CAEC had at least 78 well-trained pilot officers, divided into two tactical squadrons, and 162 NCO mechanics.

The Gibara expedition

On 17 August 1931, General Mario Menocal and Colonel Carlos Mendieta organised an uprising against President Machado, but both were arrested. For their part, the Cuban exiles in New York who supported this uprising sent an expedition to Gibara in the Cuban province of Oriente, led by Carlos Hevía, Emilio Laurent and Sergio Carbo. They immediately took over the train, telephone and telegraph stations, as well as the entrances to the town, and handed out rifles to fifty locals who joined the uprising, although none of them knew how to use them.

Some reinforcements arrived during the night under the command of Colonel Lico Galán of the so-called Liberation Army to provide support and distribute weapons and ammunition. The next day a detachment of the rural guard arrived from the town of Holguín, followed immediately after by infantry, artillery and cavalry from nearby units. The cruiser *Patria* of the Cuban navy and CAEC Vought Corsair and Curtiss P-6S Hawk fighter planes under the command of Captain Torres Menier were sent to Gibara, which was attacked by land, air and sea. The rebel leader Emilio Laurent shot down three of the attacking aircraft with his anti-aircraft gun, but the situation for the expedition members was untenable, with

CAEC Vought O2U Corsair pilots in 1929. (Vintage Cuba)

The cruiser *Patria* of the Cuban Navy (above) (Rogali Archives). A row of five CAEC Vought Corsair fighters (below). (Historia de la Avición Militar Cubana, HAMC)

government forces enjoying a twenty-to-one superiority, along with better weapons and military training. The rebels then discussed what to do, whether to break the government siege and flee to Holguín, retreat to the hills, or remain where they were in Gibara. A lack of discipline posed a serious problem for them.

The rebels were eventually forced to surrender to the much superior government forces on the 19th, having suffered six dead and 25 injured. They arrived in Havana on the 27th and were interned in the La Cabaña military prison. If the Gibara expedition was a military failure, it nevertheless served as a trigger and catalyst for subsequent revolutionary movements. Militarily, the rebel invasion of Gibara was defeated by the effective use of military aviation, which employed four Vought Corsairs and five Curtiss P-6S Hawks. In the process, the CAEC lost three aircraft shot down by anti-aircraft fire – two Corsairs and one P-6S Hawk.

The CAEC goodwill flight to Central America

Between 10 September and 3 October 1933, three CAEC Corsairs, serial numbers 27, 31 and 32, flown by Capt Mario Torres Menier, Lt Pablo Alonso and Lt Rodolfo Herrera, along with three mechanics, carried out a goodwill flight through Central America and the Southern United States starting from Havana. The flight was successfully completed. The successful flight was marked by having images of three historic Central American figures painted on the Corsairs' fuselages.

The CAEC and the Revolution of 1933

In January 1933, the CAEC received four Curtiss Wright 35A Hawk I fighters ordered the year before and priced new from the factory at US$12,600 each. They subsequently received serial numbers 19 to 22.

Two of the four CAEC Curtiss-Wright 35A Hawk 1 fighters at Camp Columbia in 1933. (Curtiss-Wright)

The CAEC had an important role in the 1933 Revolution that finally overthrew President Machado. Although the military had supported the president just two years earlier, widespread discontent in the Cuban Armed Forces led to a plan to oust him from power. Colonel Julio Sanguily and the U.S. military attaché Lieutenant Colonel T. N. Gimperling were instrumental in organising the Cuban military, including the aviation corps, for the coup. On 11 August of that year, several military units rebelled against Machado, who tried to counter the uprising with police troops. Sanguily responded by threatening to bomb government targets if Machado did not resign. Captain Torres Menier, then head of the CAEC, also demanded that President Machado resign. He finally did so on 12 August, immediately after seeing combat aircraft crewed by Menier, Laborde and Martull fly over Havana. Machado thereupon fled by air to Nassau, Bahamas, while collaborators of the deposed president were arrested and even murdered by mobs.

Upon Machado's fall, Carlos Manuel de Céspedes y Quesada assumed the presidency but was also forced to resign when, in September 1933, the Sergeants' Revolt, led by Army Sergeant Fulgencio Batista, installed a short-lived 'Pentarchy', or five-man coalition, which was replaced in turn by the so-called One Hundred Days' Government under Ramón Grau (1933-1934). On 8 November of that year, the CEAC bombed the presidential palace in an effort to oust President Grau, but the uprising was quelled by army troops. In any case, the Grau government would also end up being overthrown, in January 1934, by the now Colonel Fulgencio

Colonel Fulgencio Batista (centre), chief of staff of the Cuban Army, decorating a young lieutenant of the CAEC before the watchful eye of Cuban president Carlos Mendieta (first from the right) in an official ceremony at Camp Columbia in 1934. (Albert Grandolini via Tom Cooper)

Batista, who had assumed control over the Cuban Armed Forces by this time. Grau was replaced by Carlos Mendieta as president, with Batista ruling behind the scenes. Thus, the long period of Batista's influence in Cuban politics during the 1940s and 1950s had begun.

Despite the disorders, the CAEC continued operating, and the following 2nd lieutenants graduated from the class of 1933 as military pilots: Pablo Alonso Echeverría, Tomás Álvarez, Víctor Bermúdez Nerey, Lucas Brihuegas, Florencio Ceballos, Fernando del Valle Díaz, Laureano García Berrocal, Belisario Hernández, Antonio Herrera Toledo, Alfredo Jiménez Alum, Juan Olivera Hermida, Manuel Horta González, Guillermo Someillán, Antonio Soto Rodríguez, Miguel Rollo Gil, Marcelino Vásquez Rodríguez, Francisco Yanez and Guillermo Solorzano.

The Leonard James Povey era

With the fall of the Machado government, the Rosenham Beam era at the CEAC came to an end, and that of Leonard James Povey began. Povey was a self-taught pilot who began his aviation career in 1922 in the U.S. Army Air Service, where he was one of the first enlisted pilots. He also worked as an acrobatic pilot in aerial circuses and was known as Upside Down Povey. In 1934, Povey took part in an airshow in Miami, where a Cuban military delegation, including Batista, was in attendance. Impressed by the Povey's abilities, Batista – through Luis Ardois, the head of the Cuban delegation – invited Povey to inspect the CEAC planes and crew. He was interviewed by Batista, and despite the fact that he did not know Spanish, the two men understood each other well enough, and Povey learned that the Cuban pilots were having difficulty flying the Curtiss Hawk I fighters. The CEAC then counted some five Curtiss P-6Ss, four Curtiss Hawk Is, eleven Vought O2U-1A Corsairs, two WACO-9s, two WACO-10s and one Aeronca C-3.

Having agreed to visit Cuba, Povey flew in a Curtiss Hawk I as soon as he arrived, and he quickly realised that despite being an excellent fighter plane, the presence of an additional 50-gallon fuel tank, installed due to its short range, rendered the aircraft incapable of performing aerobatics. He was thereupon hired to reorganise the CAEC, being conferred with the rank of captain, as well as being named Batista's personal pilot. They agreed on a salary of US$7,500 per year along with a house with two servants and three cars and a driver.

For the first few months, Povey's duties were limited to performing aerial demonstrations for Batista, who told Povey that his 'job was guaranteed as long as he was in power'. Povey's organisational activities at the CAEC included selecting mechanics who were in the best physical condition to become pilots. He eventually managed to train a total of 45 pilots during his four-year stay in Cuba. When the crew of the cruiser *Cuba* mutinied, Povey, piloting a Curtiss Hawk I, flew low over the ship's deck so that the entire crew could clearly see that it was armed with bombs under the wings. He thereupon dropped the bombs near the cruiser, convincing the crew to surrender.

On 4 August 1934, the communists held a demonstration in Havana without government permission. Colonel Batista ordered the CAEC to intimidate the protesters, so a Curtiss Hawk I armed with dud 120-pound bombs was sent to make a demonstration. The aircraft, flown by Povey himself, descended from 1,000 feet and made a low pass over the communists, who, believing it was going to attack them, fled in terror. On 11 August, during a formation flight over Havana with eight planes, the Curtiss Hawk CAEC 19 that Povey was piloting collided with a large bird, a Turkish vulture, and despite his desperate attempts to parachute, he only succeeded when he was more than a mile from the city, over the sea. Batista personally visited Pavey in the hospital and decorated him after this accident.

In 1935, together with Lieutenant Manuel Horta, Povey flew the only WACO S3HD-A in the CAEC inventory. It had serial number 23 and came direct from the WACO aircraft factory in Troy, Ohio.

In 1936, the following pilot officers graduated from the Military Aviation School: Efraín García D'Abrigeon, José A. Fernández

Captain Leonard James Povey posing with his acrobatic Curtiss 35A Hawk I, serial number 21, decorated with a depiction of the Taino chieftain, Hatuey. (Nuestra Fuerza Aérea Histórica)

Martínez, Ángel González Rojas, Francisco Gutiérrez Vásques, Roberto Henderson Bezanilla, Luis Insúa, Carlos Pacual Pinar, Domingo Piñero Corno, Manuel Rebosos Brito, Guillermo Someillán González and Marcelino Vásques Rodríguez.

In 1937 the WACO S3HD-A, together with a Curtiss Hawk I with serial number 22, was flown to Missouri to participate in the St Louis Air Races. Povey placed fourth due to his Hawk I suffering engine failure during the exhibition. As for the WACO S3HD-A, it crashed in 1940 and was rendered inoperable.

Povey's aerobatics constituted one of the highlights during the fourth anniversary celebrations of the revolution on 4 September 1937. Flying his now-exclusive Curtiss Hawk I, serial number 21, adorned with a depiction of the Taino chieftain, Hatuey, along with the colours of the 1933 revolution, Povey wrote with a smoke trail in the sky the phrase Vive Batista para Cuba (Batista lives for Cuba). That same year, in December, he won first place in the 10th Annual American Air Maneuvers held in Miami, presenting his manoeuvre that later became known worldwide: the so-called *Ocho Cubano* (Cuban Eight).[1]

Captain Leonard Povey posing in front of the CAEC Waco S3HD with serial number 23. The aircraft is also adorned with a depiction of the Taino chieftain Hatuey on the fuselage. (National Waco Club)

The only Waco S3HD-A in the CEAC inventory. It had serial number 23. (National WACO Club)

After four years in Cuba, Povey decided to return to the United States in 1938. Batista offered him the Curtiss Hawk I, serial number 21, as a gift, but Povey politely refused. The friendship between Batista and Povey naturally aroused the envy of many Cubans, with reports that Povey's salary was second only to Batista's! Nevertheless, Povey continued to advise Batista and was seen at the presidential palace on the eve of Batista's overthrow in 1959. Not surprisingly, Povey was number eight on Fidel Castro's revolutionaries' most wanted list.

New reorganisation of the CAEC

By 1937, the CAEC was in urgent need of more combat aircraft, as it possessed only four Corsairs and three Hawk Is. During this period, some NCOs were accepted for pilot training after having passed the requisite physical and mental examinations.

Between 1933 and 1939, the CAEC acquired several second-hand aircraft, including an ex-Compañía Cubana de Aviación Curtiss Robin, a Bellanca 66-75 Airbus armed with two fixed .30-calibre machine guns installed in the landing gear and another in the rear part of the fuselage, in addition to having two underwing bomb racks capable of carrying a 200 lb bomb load, and six Waco biplanes, including an S3HD-2, a PCF-2, a UBF-2, a PBF-2, a CPF-6 and a ZPF-6, all of them for training and observation purposes. All of them were acquired through an American broker, and some of the aircraft were brought to Cuba in ferry flights with Povey as their pilot. A Stinson SR-9D Reliant was also acquired along with five Curtiss CW-19R all-metal aircraft. Three of the latter took part in a goodwill flight to Mexico on 10 September 1938, with a similar flight to Colombia taking place on 12 December of that year. The Curtisses were outfitted with extra ventral fuel tanks for both flights.

The CAEC also suffered losses during these years. On 11 July 1938, a CAEC Consolidated PT-3 Husky, serial number 9, flown by Lt Luis E. Insúa and Private Jesús Borrero Alfaro, crashed in the sea near Havana Beach in Baracoa due to an engine malfunction. Both crew members were killed. Meanwhile, the last Hawk I fighter in service, serial number 21, was lost when it crashed against a parked Beech D.17, registration number NC14404, during an air show at Rancho Boyeros Airport near Havana on 14 January 1939. Its pilot, Capt. Manuel Horta, was killed.

The last aircraft acquisitions in the pre-World War II period occurred between July 1939 and March 1940. They involved the purchase of seven Stearman Model A73B1 training and multipurpose aircraft, armed with three .30-calibre machine guns – two forward and one in the rear cockpit.

On the left, a CAEC Stinson SR-9 Reliant, serial number 104, along with two similar aircraft, one from Cuban naval aviation and a civilian aircraft. The odd-looking aircraft on the right is a CEAC Bellanca 66-75 Airbus with serial number 103. (San Diego Aerospace Museum)

Top: In 1939, the CAEC acquired seven Stearman Model A73B1s for primary training. (P.R.B.J. Collection)

Centre: FAEC Curtiss-Wright CW-19R, serial number 50, with its engine cowling and main landing gear spats painted in bright red. (San Diego Aerospace Museum Collection)

Bottom: CAEC Curtiss-Wright CW-19R, serial number 51 (left). Lt Enrique Carreras Rolas in the front seat of a CW-19R in 1945 (right). (San Diego Aerospace Museum & P.R.B.J. Collection)

3

THE CAEC IN WORLD WAR II AND THE LEND-LEASE PROGRAM

In September 1939, the CAEC, which was under the command of Colonel Otalio Soca Llanes during the war years, increased the number of pilots assigned to its tactical squadrons, with each squadron receiving an additional five officers. The corps comprised two combat squadrons at that time: the *Escuadrón de Observación y Bombardeo* (Observation and Bombardment Squadron) and the *Escuadrón de Persecución* (Pursuit Squadron). The squadrons possessed a variety of aircraft acquired in the 1930s, including Corsairs, Hawks and CW-19Rs. More pilots joined both squadrons by December.

In 1939, the following officers graduated as military pilots: José A. Alonso, Miguel A. Alonso Estévez, Benigno Díaz Doval, Francisco Fernández Bernaza, José A. Fernández Martínez, Jorge González Rojas, Luis González Rojas, Ángel Gutiérrez Vásquez, Mario León González, Celso Mancitos, Luis Palacios and Manuel Reboso Brito.

On 3 June 1940, the so-called ANACRA – the National Academy of Civil Aviation – was created, which functioned as an air reserve for the CAEC, employing military instructors to train civilian pilots. In 1943, the CAEC transferred its four Aeronca 65TCs to the academy. The first class of civilian pilots numbered 150 men, with the training flights carried out at the *Comandante Manuel Pérez Alfonso* Camp at Rancho Boyeros airport. Politically, 1940 saw the resignation of President Federico Laredo Bru. In his place, Fulgencio Batista ran as a candidate for the Democratic Socialist Coalition in the 1940 elections and emerged victorious. His first term as president began on 10 October of that year.

In 1941, the following officers graduated from the Military Aviation School as pilots: Alfredo Acosta Iglesias, Benito Aldecocea López, Juventino Báez Rodríguez, Gastón Bernal Fernández, Julio Caballero García, Agustín Cartaya, Jorge Casales Escarras, Jorge Casanova Pellicer, Felipe Catasús Pazos, Francisco Cuadra Aguirre, Alberto Dávila Sala, Jorge Escobar Quesada, Alfredo Fernández Nespral, Eduardo Ferrer del Castillo, José E. García D'Abrigeon, Antonio González Torrecilla, Ángel Gutiérrez Vásquez, Heriberto Hernández Nevares, Manuel Martínez Saladrigas, Máximo Pruna Hernández, Pedro Roque Lazar, Víctor San Julián Casas, Alfonso Silva Tablada, René Somodevilla, Carlos M. Tabernilla Palmero, Jorge Triana Díaz and Lorenzo Triana Roche.

Cuba enters the war

On 9 December 1941, just two days after the Japanese attack on Pearl Harbor, Cuba declared war on Japan. Two days later, it did the same against Germany and Italy. ANACRA was incorporated into the Ministry of Defence, and all civilian pilot graduates became part of the CAEC air reserve.

An aerial view of Rancho Boyeros airport near Havana in the early 1940s (left). The Rancho Boyeros airport terminal building with four *Cubana de Aviación* DC-3s and a Pan American C-46 on the tarmac (right). (Open source)

The CAEC received 6 Boeing-Stearman PT-17 Kaydets through the U.S. Lend-Lease Program in July 1942. (Albert Grandolini via Tom Cooper & Vintage Cuba)

The CAEC also received 6 Vultee BT-13A Valiants through the Lend-Lease Program between September and October 1942. On the right, a young Lieutenant Enrique Carreras Rolas poses in front of a Vultee BT-13. Rolas would become one of the legendary pilots in the Rebel Air Force and later in the Revolutionary Air Force (FAR). (Reproduction from the book *Por El Dominio del Aire* by Enrique Carreras Rolas)

A CAEC North American AT-6C Texan, serial number 106, armed with bombs on a patrol flight over the Caribbean Sea during World War II. Nine AT-6Cs were delivered to the CAEC through the Lend-Lease Program between October 1942 and June 1943 (top) (P.R.B.J. Collection). A CAEC AT-6C taking off on a routine training mission in the mid-1940s (bottom). (Albert Grandolini collection via Tom Cooper)

During World War II, some CAEC AT-6s received olive green camouflage. In a photo obviously staged for propaganda purposes, Colonel Soca Llanes gives instructions to CAEC pilots before a patrol mission in the Gulf of Mexico with AT-6s during World War II. (Albert Grandolini Archives via Tom Cooper)

A group of CAEC aviation mechanic sergeants pose with some pilots in front of a Stearman PT-17 during World War II. Note a Beech C-45 in the background. (Albert Grandolini Archives via Tom Cooper)

A CAEC Aeronca L-3B, serial number 5, looking very aggressive with a painted shark's mouth at Camp Columbia, near Havana. Note a Stearman PT-17 and an AT-6C in the background. Six of these Aeroncas were received in May 1943 through the Lend-Lease Program. (Nuestra Fuerza Aérea Histórica)

One of the ten North American AT-6F Texans delivered to the CAEC between May and June 1945 through the Lend-Lease Program. This photo was taken in 1955 when the traditional insignia of the CAEC was changed. (P.R.B.J. Collection)

The CAEC contributed to the Allied cause during the war by carrying out anti-submarine patrol missions in the Caribbean and the Gulf of Mexico, employing both North American Aviation T-6C Texan trainers and Curtiss-Wright CW-19 utility aircraft, with the T-6Cs operating out of air bases in the towns of Ciego de Ávila and Preston. Missions were carried out especially in the area of the Nicaro nickel mines, which were so vital to the war effort. Indeed, one T-6C, with serial number 102, was lost during one of those long patrol missions. Nevertheless, German submarines sank four Cuban merchant ships – Mambi, Manzanillo, Santiago and Libertad – with various cargo, killing 56 Cuban sailors.

Given the strategic importance of Cuba's geographic location in the Caribbean and the Gulf of Mexico, the CAEC greatly benefited from the U.S. Lend-Lease Program. Between 1942 and 1945, the CAEC received 43 training aircraft (*) which completely renewed the old air fleet from the 1930s, namely:

Table 1: Lend-Lease aircraft delivered to the CAEC[1]

Date	Model	Quantity	USAAF serial	CAEC serial
July 1942	Boeing-Stearman PT-17 Kaydet	6	41-25741 41-25743 41-25744 41-25745 41-25746 41-25747	38 39 40 41 42 43
September-October 1942	Vultee BT-13A Valiant	6	41-22673 41-22674 41-22675 41-22795 41-22896 41-22797	66 67 68 69 70 71
October-November 1942	North American AT-6C Texan	6	41-32403 41-32404 41-32405 41-32528 41-32529 41-32530	102 103 104 105 106 107
February 1943	Vultee BT-13A Valiant	3	42-42302 42-42303 42-42304	72 73 74
May 1943	Aeronca L-3B	6	43-26764 43-26769 43-26774 43-26776 43-26778 43-26780	1 2 3 4 5 6
June 1943	North American AT-6C Texan	3	42-4234 42-4235 42-4236	108 109 110
June 1943	Boeing-Stearman N2S-4	3	42-16274 42-16275 42-16276	44 45 46
May-June 1945	North American AT-6F Texan	10	44-81913 44-81914 44-81915 44 81916 44-81917 44-81040 44-81041 44-81042 44-81043 44-81944	111 112 113 114 115 116 117 118 119 120

(*) Five of the eleven Aeronca L-3Bs were not delivered.

In addition to the aircraft already mentioned, the Lend-Lease Program also delivered 5 Curtiss SNC-1 fighters in order to supplement the already existing CW-19Rs in the CAEC, which had been acquired in 1937. The SNC-1s arrived at Camp Columbia in July 1942, but they were not accepted by the CAEC since they were not equipped with the required engines and ordnance, so they were redelivered to Venezuela. Non-Lend-Lease acquisitions included a Beechcraft S.17D Staggerwing which was confiscated from Senator Emilio Ochoa towards the end of the war and was used as VIP transport until the 1950s, and two Stinsons – a 105 gifted by Mrs Celia Velazco and a 108 acquired for the same purpose. Upon the end of the war, in 1946, the CAEC would acquire an additional three Boeing-Stearman N2S-4 Kaydet primary trainers to replace the operational losses.

During World War II, many CAEC pilot officers received training at Kelly Field and Randolph Field in Texas in order to become flight instructors in Cuba. They were also trained in night flying and IFR instrument flying. It is estimated that with the aircraft transferred to the CAEC through the Lend-Lease Program, at least 93 new pilots were able to successfully complete their flight training during the war years, including nighttime and instrument training.

On 12 February 1943, six CAEC AT-6Cs carried out a goodwill flight to Mexico City, where they remained for 17 days. They gave demonstration flights, and their crews interacted with their Mexican Air Force peers. In June of that year, another goodwill flight to Mexico took place, this time with three AT-6Cs crewed by captains Roberto Henderson Besanilla, Laureano García Berrocal and Francisco Gutiérrez, along with sergeant mechanics Barrios and Delfín Burlas. The second crew member on the aircraft flown by Captain Henerson was Colonel Otalio Soca Llanes, head of the CAEC.

The class of military pilots of 1943 was made up of the following CAEC officers: Jorge Alemany Peláez, Ramón Alonso Guillot, Néstor Álvarez Fernández, Enrique Becalli, Mario Cabréras Bosque, Enrique Carreras Rolas, José M. Castellanos Reyes Gavilán, Roberto Cendoya Echevarría, Guillermo Corvo Alzamora, José de la Peña García, Oscar del Valle Cabieris, Enrique Domínguez Pérez, Mario Dutil Somodevilla, Humberto Hernández Nevares, Jorge Foyo González, Rolando García Báez, Juan A. García Rodríguez, Leopoldo Infante Fernández, Luis Larrea González, Rafael Lima Silva, Tomás Lingoya y González Clave, Vilorio Mata, Miguel Matamoros del Valle, José Matos Méstre, Hubert Masmontet Pompeidin Cuervo, Rogelio Miró Quirós, Juan Olivera Hermida, Pablo Palmero Diehl, Luis Pérez Escandón, Jorge Perramón Spencer, Agustín Piñera Machín, Carlos Pirri Llorca, Ernesto Puig Miyar, Manuel Ramírez Sotto, Marcelo Tabernilla Palmero, Cosme A. Varas Castro, Manuel Vidal Méndez and Ricardo Zorrilla Armenteros.

For its part, the Cuban Navy also actively participated in World War II in its area of competence. On 15 May 1943, the Cuban submarine chaser SC-13, with the help of American Kingfisher aircraft, sank the German submarine U-176 with two depth charges, killing its entire 53-man crew along with its captain, Reiner Dierksen, near the province of Matanzas. In 1944, Cuba requested the delivery of at least 10 Douglas A-24B Dauntless dive bombers as part of the Lend-Lease Program in order to reinforce their ocean patrol missions, but the request was rejected. The same happened with their request for 6 Vultee A-35B Vengeances, 6 North American B-25 Mitchells and a single Cessna UC-78 Bobcat.

USAAF bases in Cuba

On 9 September 1942, Cuba and the United States signed a military and naval cooperation agreement. Cuba's strategic importance for U.S. maritime and air communications as well as its sugar industry were key elements in the U.S. decision to reinforce the island's defences. During the World War II years, the U.S. Army Corps of Engineers built two all-weather airports in Cuba, one at San Antonio de los Baños in Havana province, which was known as La Cayuga, a nickname given it because of the name of the construction company that built the airport, and the other at San Julián in Guanacabides in Pinar del Rio province. The airport at San Antonio was later named Batista Field, in recognition of the assistance provided by President Fulgencio Batista. The USAAF established air bases at these airports, equipped with Bell P-39 Airacobra fighters, Douglas B-18 Bolo medium bombers, Lockheed B-34 Ventura patrol bombers and

During World War II, USAAF aircraft operated in Cuba out of the San Antonio de los Baños airport. This photo shows four American B-24 Liberators flying over the San Carlos de la Cabaña fortress in Havana. (Nuestra Fuerza Aérea Histórica)

Consolidated B-24D Liberator bombers. American aircraft were able to use these bases to carry out patrols along the Cuban coasts, hunting down German submarines, with the USAAF using the San Antonio de los Baños base and the U.S. Navy operating out of the one in San Julián.

The bases, as well as the airports in Camagüey and Camp Columbia near Havana, also served as mandatory stopover points for bombers that were being deployed to the European theatre of operations. By the end of 1944, a training ground was already being established for the USAAF 509th Composite Group for training crews for Boeing B-29 Superfortress heavy bombers. Both American-built airports were subsequently transferred to the Cuban Army at the end of the war during the second Ramón Grau San Martín presidency (1944-1948), following the end of Batista's first term. The San Antonio base was used by the CAEC, while the San Julián base was turned into an aviation mechanics' school.

The U.S. Navy military air base at San Julián in Pinar del Río province. The photo shows five Vought Kingfishers, a Cessna UC-78 Bobcat, a Grumman G-21 Goose, a North American AT-6C and a Lockheed PV-2 Harpoon. (U.S. Navy Archives)

Two CAEC Boeing-Stearman N2S-4 Kaydets acquired in 1946. (Historia de la Aviación Militar Cubana, HAMC)

Aircraft built in Cuba

In addition to the aforementioned Comas aerial velocipede of 1893, there were other attempts to build aircraft in Cuba. As early as 1911, Joaquín Lazaga and Benigno Carvajal built a primitive biplane that they called the *Cuba*. Lack of official support, mainly for the acquisition of a 40 hp Curtiss engine, which would have powered the plane, stymied their efforts, however. In 1941, Eugenio Hernández Álvarez designed a glider, subsequently known as the 'Hernández Glider', whose construction began in July of that year but would be completed only in 1945 in the city of Cárdenas. Several flights were thereupon carried out at the end of the year with Hernández himself and Pedro de la Fe Flores at the controls, and certification was subsequently obtained from the Cuban Aeronautical Federation. The glider was finally presented to the Cuban press in January 1946. The machine was pulled by a Ford car with a 450-metre-long rope until it took off and freed itself from the rope, ascending to an initial height of 250 metres. The glider, making use of thermal currents, then ascended and remained in the air for 23 minutes before finally making a perfect landing.

The Cuban experimental aircraft *Estrella Errante*, registration number CUX-143, photographed in 1948 at Camp Columbia (left). Note the CAEC P-38M, serial number 125, behind it to the left, along with two B-25s further in the distance (Rod Simpson). The *Cuba* biplane built in 1911 (top right) and Hernández's glider in 1945 (bottom right). (Aviación Cubana)

The next attempt at domestic aircraft design was made in 1942 when CAEC officers Major Benigno Díaz y Doval, Lieutenant Jorge Merlo and Lieutenant Roberto Gode built a parasol wing monoplane, which they called *Estrella Errante* (Wandering Star). The aeroplane was built in Camagüey but crashed and was damaged during its maiden flight while taking off from a precarious runway. It is thought that it was repaired afterwards since a photo taken later in 1948 shows the aircraft in good shape. The machine was granted the Cuban civil registration number CUX-143.

CAEC accidents in the mid-1940s

The increase in flights during the period 1943-1945 brought with it several accidents. On 5 February 1943, Lt Néstor Hernández was seriously injured when his Aeronca L-3B, serial number 4, crashed in Finca Central Toledo. On 21 July that same year, Captain Roberto Roque and Sergeant Fernando Cuba were killed when their Vultee BT-13, serial number 72, crashed while coming out of a dive over the Guines area of Havana. In another serious accident involving a Vultee BT-13, the then head of the CEAC, Major Manuel Pérez Alonso, was killed when the plane he and his instructor, Captain Efraín Hernández D'Abrignon, were in and another similar aircraft piloted by a Cadet Somodevilla collided with some hills near the town of Artemisa, in Pinar del Rio. Cadet Somodevilla was also killed in the crash, but Captain Hernández survived, although with serious injuries. He would never fly again.

On 20 November 1943, an AT-6C with serial number 102 crashed in Finca Grande near Concepción; its crew – lieutenants Antonio González Torres and José Fernández Saborit – were seriously injured. In March 1944, Lieutenant José Rodríguez was killed instantly when his ANACRA Aeronca 65TC crashed in Rancho Boyeros. In May of that same year, Lieutenant Pepín Fernández suffered minor injuries when his Vultee BT-13 crashed when caught in a crosswind while approaching the runway at Central Steward. The same month, Lieutenant Vasquez and his instructor, Captain Palacios, were killed when their Curtiss CW-19R, serial number 101, crashed in Toledo, near Havana. Lieutenant Larin also lost his life when his AT-6C was involved in an accident at the Maisi airstrip.

On 16 July 1945, Lieutenants Zorrilla and Henderson were killed when their Beechcraft F-2B, serial number 212, crashed when they were approaching Charleston, South Carolina, on their return flight from Washington D.C. to Cuba. Their passenger, Major Rivero – an assistant to the head of the Cuban Army – was also killed. The other aircraft in that flight, a Beechcraft UC-45F, serial number 213, flown by Lieutenant Fernández, arrived in Cuba safely together with its passenger, the head of the Cuban Army, General Genovevo Pérez Damera.

Cuban pilots who fought overseas during World War II

As with many other Latin American countries, numerous Cubans went to fight during the Second World War, joining the armed forces of various countries. Two of the more well-known pilots of Cuban origin in World War II were:

- **William Ralph Perez** was born in Havana, Cuba, on 3 September 1921. He attended high school in the United States and joined the U.S. Army Air Corps (USAAC) at the age of 20. There he received training as a fighter pilot with the Lockheed P-38 Lightning. As first lieutenant, he was sent to Europe to carry out missions with the 343rd Squadron of the 8th Air Force, escorting B-17 Flying Fortresses over Germany. Perez completed 270 hours of combat duty, shooting down five enemy planes in the process. He was known as *El As Cubano* (the Cuban Ace) and was awarded the Distinguished Flying Cross (DFC). Perez was killed in an accident involving a P-51 Mustang during a routine flight in Maracay, Venezuela, on 25 November 1946. He was 26.

- **Miguel 'Mike' Enciso Seiglie** joined the Royal Canadian Air Force (RCAF) in 1942 and was sent to England to join the 1st Bomber Group in 1944. He arrived in Liverpool in January 1944, receiving the rank of flying officer (first lieutenant) with the RAF. As a member of the 1st Bomber Group, Seiglie flew a Lancaster BX on bombing missions over Berlin, Nuremberg, Kassel, Mannheim and targets in the Baltic Sea. In the course of his bombing runs, he was shot several times by enemy planes and artillery, and on one occasion he had to make a forced landing after losing a landing gear when attacked by a Luftwaffe Focke-Wulf 190 fighter. On the night of 9 April, 1945, he was responsible for the sinking of the German heavy cruiser *Admiral Scheer*, whose deck he managed to hit with a Tallboy bomb, setting the ship on fire and causing it to capsize later. He followed this up with bombing raids against enemy submarines moored in the port of Kiel. For the sinking of the *Admiral Scheer*, he was awarded five medals, including a special decoration from King George VI. Seiglie entered commercial aviation after the war, becoming a pilot of a Bristol Britannia four-engine turboprop airliner with *Cubana de Aviación*. During a stopover in Gander in Canada on one of these flights, he requested asylum and remained living in the country until his death.

First Lieutenant William Ralph Perez, a Cuban pilot serving in the USAAF, being decorated with the Distinguished Flying Cross at the end of World War II (left). A Lockheed P-38H-1-LO of the 343rd Fighter Squadron of the 8th AF similar to the one flown by Perez (right). (USAAF Archives)

First Lieutenant Miguel Enciso Siegle, a Cuban pilot serving in the RCAF during World War II (top left). Lt Enciso Siegle with his crew atop their Avro Lancaster bomber (top right) (RCAF Archives). Seiglie and his crew were responsible for sinking the German heavy cruiser *Admiral Scheer*. (bottom). (Internet)

4

FULGENCIO BATISTA ZALDÍVAR (1901-1973)

Early life

Fulgencio Batista was born Rubén Fulgencio Batista Zaldívar on 16 January 1901 into a family with very limited resources. He was the first of four sons born to Belisario Batista Palermo and Carmela Zaldívar Gonzáles in the town of Veguitas in Banes municipality in Cuba's northeastern Oriente province. Belisario Batista had fought in the Cuban War of Independence against Spain under General Jose Maceo and was a sugarcane cutter employed by a local contractor for the United Fruit Company. The family was poor, and the relationship between Fulgencio Batista and his father was not good, so Fulgencio took it upon himself to raise, educate, and care for his younger brothers Juan (b. 1905), Hermelindo (b. 1906), and Francisco (b. 1911).

Fulgencio began studying first at a public school in Banes and then, at the age of ten, at an American Quaker school in the same city in September 1911. Most Cuban students were taught in Spanish, and Batista graduated in 1913 with a fourth-grade education. He then worked in the sugarcane fields with his father. During the off-season, he worked in a variety of small jobs in town, including as an apprentice to a barber and a tailor. His mother died in 1916, and in the following year, at age 15, Fulgencio Batista ran away from home.

Joining the military

Between 1916 and 1921, Batista was frequently destitute and often homeless and travelled about while working at an odd assortment of jobs, including mechanic, charcoal vendor and fruit peddler,

Fulgencio Batista when he was eight years old in Banes, Holguín (left). A very young Batista, when he worked at the *Ferrocarriles del Norte* railway in the province of Camagüey in the early 1920s (centre). Batista in a photo studio with a suit and bowtie also in the 1920s (right). (Open source)

Sergeant Fulgencio Batista (third from the right) with several Cuban Army NCOs and some civilians in the late 1920s. (Rogali collection)

until getting a job with the *Ferrocarriles del Norte* railways in Camagüey Province. He sent money home when he could but was nearly killed in an accident at the railroad that left him hospitalised for several weeks and scarred him for life. Although there were late-night parties, drinking, and womanising among the railway employees, Batista rarely attended and was remembered instead as a voracious reader.

On 15 April 1921, Batista enlisted in the Cuban Army as a private and joined the 4th Infantry Regiment of the First Battalion in Camp Columbia, Havana. After learning shorthand and typing, Batista left the army, working briefly as a teacher of stenography before enlisting in the *Guardia Rural* in 1923. The *Guardia Rural* was a branch of the army endowed with police functions in the countryside. On 10 July 1926, he married Elisa Godínez Gómez (1905–1993), and they would have three children (Fulgencio Ruben, Mirta Caridad, and Elisa Aleida). Batista was first promoted to corporal in 1927 and then transferred back to the army, where he became a secretary to a regimental colonel. In 1928, he was promoted to sergeant. In September 1933, he held the rank of first sergeant stenographer and, as such, acted as the secretary of a group of non-commissioned officers who led the 'Sergeants' Revolt' aimed at bettering living conditions and improving the prospects of promotion. He worked as an army stenographer for General Machado's chief of staff, General Herrera.

Sergeant Batista becomes a dominant political figure

Batista was a young sergeant in the army when the repressive government of General Gerardo Machado fell apart in 1933. The charismatic Batista organised the so-called 'Sergeants' Revolt' of non-commissioned officers and seized control of the armed forces. By making alliances with student groups and unions, Batista was able to put himself in a position where he was effectively ruling the country. He eventually broke with the student groups, including the Revolutionary Directorate (a student activist group), and they became his implacable enemies. Machado was finally overthrown on 12 August 1933, and he fled the country to the Bahamas.

The new government of Carlos Manuel de Céspedes y Quesada was unable to achieve firm control over the country, and so Batista and the other sergeants began conspiring again. On 4 September, the sergeants rebelled once more, with Batista as the dominant figure. Some officers also joined the cause, in addition to numerous civilians. A short-lived five-member presidency, known as the Pentarchy of 1933, was thereupon established. The Pentarchy included a representative from each anti-Machado faction. Batista was not a member, but he controlled Cuba's armed forces. Within days, the representative for the students and professors of the University of Havana, Ramón Grau San Martín, was made president, and Batista

Sergeant Batista (centre) with army comrades and civilian leaders of the 1933 Revolution (left). Army Sergeant Fulgencio Batista in the early 1930s (right). (Open source)

Sergeant Batista with his first wife, Elisa Godínez Gómez, and their first two children (left). Batista hugging the new president of Cuba, Ramón Grau San Martín, after the coup that overthrew Machado. (Open source)

became the army chief of staff, with his meteoric rise to the rank of colonel, effectively putting him in control of the presidency.

Prior to his promotion to colonel, a conflict had broken out between the officers who had been expelled from the army and the NCOs commanded by Batista. The first barricaded themselves in the National Hotel with weapons, and on 2 October 1933, the battle began, resulting in around 200 deaths in that area of the city. Some CAEC pilots also joined the rebel officers, strafing Batista's NCOs from their aircraft, which caused more casualties. The conflict was not only in Havana but broke out in several other cities as well. Nevertheless, Batista was able to reduce the rebels with his troops, obtaining support both from the navy and from the CAEC.

The 'Sergeants' Revolt' was led by quartermaster sergeants Pablo Rodriguez and Manuel López Migoya, First Sergeant José E. Pedraza and Major Sergeant Fulgencio Batista. After the revolution, Rodriguez became a major, Pedraza and Batista became colonels, and Migoya a lieutenant colonel. Moreover, when hundreds of officers who did not support the uprising retired, 28 non-commissioned officers, 363 sergeants, 28 corporals and also 32 privates were also promoted to the rank of officers. Some 112 officers supported the insurrection, the majority being captains and lieutenants, who, of course, continued on with their military careers.

Right: Fulgencio Batista enjoyed a meteoric rise in rank from sergeant to that of colonel, becoming the head of the Cuban Army. (Open source)

Below: The head of the Cuban Army, Colonel Fulgencio Batista (centre), with the president of Cuba, Federico Laredo Bru (with dark glasses), in March 1937. (Rogali collection)

Grau remained president for just over 100 days before Batista, conspiring with the U.S. envoy Sumner Welles, forced him to resign in January 1934. Grau was replaced by Carlos Mendieta, and within five days the U.S. had recognised Cuba's new government, which lasted eleven months. Batista then became the strongman behind a succession of puppet presidents until he was elected president in 1940. After Mendieta, succeeding governments were led by José Agripino Barnet (five months) and Miguel Mariano Gómez (seven months) before Federico Laredo Brú ruled from December 1936 to October 1940.

Batista's first presidential term, 1940–1944

In 1938, Batista ordered a new constitution, and in order to run for the presidency of the country, he retired from the army. In 1940, he was elected president in a somewhat crooked election, defeating Grau, with his party also winning a majority in Congress. Batista was endorsed by the Democratic Socialist Coalition and the original Cuban Communist Party (later known as the Popular Socialist Party), which at the time had little significance and no probability of an electoral victory. This support was primarily due to Batista's early advocacy of strengthening labour laws and his support for labour unions, with which the Communists had close ties, as well as his pro-Allied stance in World War II. In fact, the Communists attacked the anti-Batista opposition, saying that Grau and the others were 'fascists' and 'reactionaries'. Batista carried out major social reforms and established numerous economic regulations and pro-union policies during his first term in office.

It was also during Batista's first term that Cuba formally entered World War II on the side of the Allies. In the following year, under the Lend-Lease Act, Cuba was granted US$7.2 million of military materiel, mainly aircraft.

In 1942, the Cuban Congress enacted a new law reorganising the army and according to which the head of the army should have the rank of major general. Batista was already retired by this time, but he was still promoted to this rank since he had been head of the army in the past. Although he presided over a relatively stable time and the economy was good, his candidate, Carlos Saladrigas Zayas, who had been chosen to succeed him in office, was defeated by Dr Ramón Grau in the 1944 elections. Batista's wife Elisa was the First Lady of Cuba, but in October 1945, he divorced her and six weeks later married Marta Fernandez Miranda (1923–2006). They would eventually have five children together (Jorge Luis, Roberto Francisco, Fulgencio Jose, Marta María and Carlos Manuel).

Return to the presidency

Batista and his new wife moved to a house in Daytona Beach in the United States and lived there for some years before deciding to re-enter Cuban politics. In fact, two of their children were born in the U.S. When he decided to participate in Cuban politics again, he was elected to the Cuban Senate *in absentia* in 1948. Returning to Cuba, he decided to run for president and received permission from President Grau, whereupon he formed the *Partido Acción Unitaria* (Unitary Action Party, PAU) in April 1949. He never regained his former popular support, though the unions supported him until the end.

Colonel Fulgencio Batista (centre) arriving in Washington D.C. in November 1938. (Rogali collection)

Fulgencio Batista on the day of his presidential inauguration in 1940 (left). Although he was retired from the army by 1942, he was promoted to the rank of major general for having been the head of the army (right). (Open source)

Opening celebrations of the San Julián Aeronautical School on 20 October 1955. President Fulgencio Batista is speaking, with special guests sitting in the front row (left to right), the minister of education, Dr Aureliano Fernández; the American ambassador, Arthur Gardner; and Dr Ellwood C. Nance, rector of the University of Tampa, among others. In the background there is a CAEC C-47 with serial number 206 (left). President Batista and his second wife, Marta Fernández Miranda (cutting the ribbon), with whom he had five children (right). (Open source)

Batista ran for president in 1952, assuming that most Cubans had missed him during his years away. In a three-way race, Roberto Agramonte of the Orthodox Party led in all the polls, followed by Carlos Hevia of the Authentic Party. Batista's United Action coalition was running a distant third. It soon became apparent that he would lose. Fearful of losing entirely his weakening grip on power, Batista and his allies in the military decided to take control of the government by force on 10 March. He ousted outgoing President Carlos Prío Socarrás, cancelled the elections and took control of the government as a provisional president. It was on this occasion that he declared to his colleagues, '*Soy yo quien determina las leyes militares. El Ejército soy yo*'[1] (I am the one who determines military laws. The Army is me.) The PAU would later change its name to the *Partido Acción Progresista* (Progressive Action Party, PAP).

Batista initially enjoyed a great deal of support. Many of his former cronies in the military had been weeded out or passed over for promotion in the years since Batista had left. It was suspected that many of these officers might have gone ahead with a takeover even if they had not convinced Batista to go along with it. In the early hours of 10 March 1952, about three months before the election was scheduled, the plotters silently took control of Camp Columbia military compound and the fort of La Cabaña. Strategic

The first combat aircraft acquired by the CAEC were nine Curtiss JN-4D Jenny biplanes, ordered in 1918 and delivered by 1924. They were withdrawn from service already by 1927 and replaced – starting in 1924 – by six de Havilland DH-4Ms, one of which is shown here. The DH-4Ms were armed with a front-firing 7.7mm Vickers machine gun and a Lewis machine gun mounted on a scarf ring in the rear cockpit. The aircraft could also carry up to 210kg of bombs. Notably, the early Cuban national markings already included the roundels (on the underside of the wings), as well as the classic tricolour applied on the rudder. (Artwork by Tom Cooper)

Also in 1924, the CAEC acquired nine Vought QO-2 Corsair two-seat fighters. Five years later, they were supplemented by six Vought O2U-1A Corsair two-seat observation and light attack aircraft, while in 1933, 11 Vought O2U-3A Corsairs were also purchased, bringing the total to 26. Cuban Corsairs saw action during the Gibara Expedition of 1931, when two were shot down by anti-aircraft fire. They were armed with three 7.62mm Browning M1919 machine guns (one firing towards the front and two in a flexible mount in the rear seat) and retained their silver dope overall finish throughout their careers. (Artwork by Luca Canossa)

In 1929, the combat component of the CAEC was reinforced through the purchase of five Curtiss P-65 Hawk fighters and two WACO 10 trainers. Meanwhile, a year earlier, the Cubans acquired 10 Consolidated PT-3 Husky biplanes to serve as primary trainers. The aircraft – one of which is shown here – were delivered in a silver dope overall colour, which they retained for the duration of their service in Cuba. Huskies were some of the first to receive the final version of the Cuban national insignia applied on their rudders. (Artwork by Luca Canossa)

Six Curtiss P-6S Hawks, acquired starting in 1929, followed by four Curtiss-Wright 35A Hawk Is, purchased in 1933, became some of the most colourful and most famous early fighter aircraft of the CAEC. The Hawk I illustrated here was the personal aircraft of Captain Leo Povey during his four-year tour in Cuba as the director of the Military Aviation School. He had it decorated with an ornate emblem representing the Taino chieftain, Hatuey; a colourful CAEC shield on the fin; and the Cuban national colours on the top of the upper and on the bottom of the lower wings. (Artwork by Luca Canossa)

The Curtiss-Wright CW-19R was a little-known two-seat fighter with an all-metal construction, five of which were acquired by Cuba in 1937. They were armed with one to three machine guns firing forward and one in a flexible mount installed in the rear cockpit. Additionally, they could carry light bombs attached to underwing hardpoints. (Artwork by Luca Canossa)

The CAEC was significantly bolstered during the Second World War, when it acquired numerous modern aircraft types through the Lend-Lease Program. Some of the first of these were five Curtiss SNC-1 fighters, acquired to supplement the existing CW-19Rs. The SNC-1s were delivered to Camp Columbia in July 1942; however, the CAEC turned them down because they were neither powered by the required engines nor outfitted with the requested ordnance. Therefore, all five were re-routed to Venezuela instead. (Artwork by Luca Canossa)

In 1942-1943, the CAEC received nine Vultee BT-13A Valiant basic trainers. This was a slightly more powerful variant of the original BT-13, equipped with an R-985-AN-1 engine and other minor changes. The Valiants proved highly reliable and popular in service and served with the Military Aviation School, which used them to accelerate training programmes and qualify a large number of new pilots and ground personnel. All were left in bare metal overall but had a big anti-glare panel in matt black along the upper section of the forward fuselage. (Artwork by Luca Canossa)

The Lend-Lease Program also brought the first North American AT-6C Texans to Cuba, with a total of nine acquired in 1942-1943. Throughout the Second World War, they were painted in olive green on the upper surfaces and sides and light grey on the undersides and flew combat air patrols. The example shown here was lost during one lengthy mission over the Caribbean. Later on, the AT-6Cs were deployed for counter-insurgency operations. The Cuban AT-6Cs were armed with two 7.62mm machine guns firing forward and a pintle-mounted machine gun in the rear cabin. They could also carry bombs and rockets on underwing hardpoints. (Artwork by Luca Canossa)

In 1945, the CAEC received 10 AT-6Fs through the Lend-Lease Program. While designed as advanced trainers, they were armed with two 7.62mm machine guns firing forward and could take a third on a pintle in the rear cabin and were deployed to fly combat air patrols over the Caribbean as well. However, unlike the AT-6Cs, they were left in their bare metal overall livery. Together with a handful of AT-6Cs, several AT-6Fs survived long enough to serve with the FAR. (Artwork by Luca Canossa)

After the Second World War, Cuba continued acquiring US-made military aircraft through the American Republics Program (ARP). Some of the first of these were 12 Douglas C-47s and one DC-3 equipped as a VIP transport, delivered between 1946 and 1956. Additionally, in 1947, following the failed Cayo Confites adventure, the CAEC received two second-hand C-47s. Early in their service life, the Cuban Dakotas retained an overall bare metal livery and wore large service titles applied high on the centre fuselage, as illustrated here. (Artwork by Luca Canossa)

In 1947, the CAEC acquired two Lockheed RB-34 Ventura patrol bombers. Both were armed with four 12.7m Browning M2 machine guns, two 7.62mm M1919 Browning machine guns, and could carry up to 1,400kg of bombs, or six 147kg depth charges or one torpedo. Both retained their bare metal overall livery but were withdrawn from service only a year later, thus remaining relatively unknown outside Cuba. (Artwork by Luca Canossa)

Starting in 1947, the CAEC's sole fighter squadron received a total of six Lockheed P-38L Lightning fighters and three P-38M night fighters, seized during the failed Cayo Confites expedition. Most of them retained their bare metal overall livery, but the P-38Ms were painted in black overall. They were armed with four 12.7mm Browning M2 machine guns and could carry three three-tube M10 launchers for 112mm unguided rockets or 900kg of bombs or drop tanks. (Artwork by Jean-Marie Guillou)

Another significant seizure during the Cayo Confites affair of 1947 was a Consolidated P4Y-1 Liberator patrol bomber. Armed with a total of eight 12.7mm Browning M2 machine guns (six of these installed in a total of three turrets) and capable of carrying up to 3,600kg bombs in its bay, the aircraft was originally left in bare metal overall livery. This rapidly dilapidated under the local climate; indeed, the sole Cuban Liberator was flown very little and was already derelict by 1948. (Artwork by Jean-Marie Guillou)

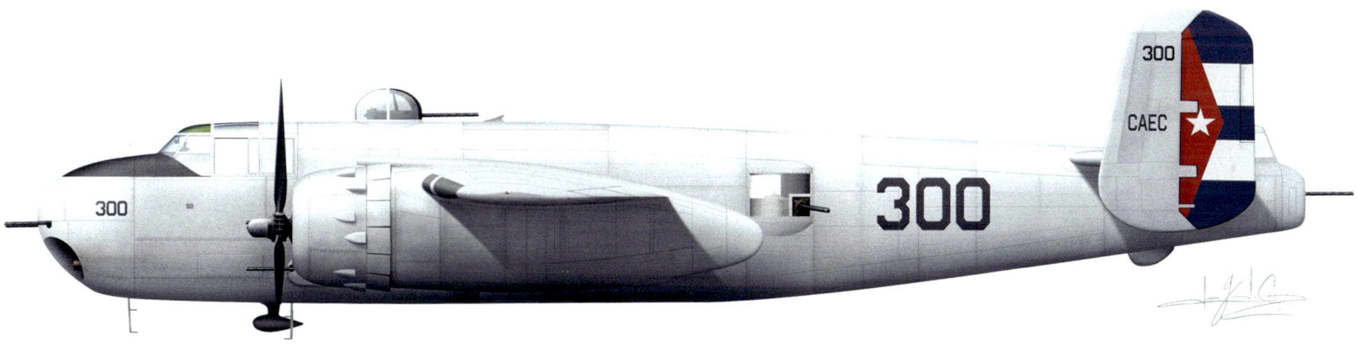

In 1947, the CAEC began acquiring North American B-25 Mitchell bombers – partially through seizures during the Cayo Confites affair and partially through the acquisitions from the U.S. The first of these was this B-25H, serial number 300, armed with a single 75mm cannon (firing forward) and one 12.7mm Browning M2 machine gun (additionally, the aircraft could load up to 1,360kg of bombs in its internal bomb bay). The aircraft served with the CAEC for 10 years, until it was sold to the Uruguayan Air Force in 1957. (Artwork by Luca Canossa)

The sole B-25H – which remained the only such Mitchell in Cuban service – was accompanied by a single B-25C acquired during the Cayo Confites affair and six B-25Js acquired through the ARP (one of which is shown here). The armament of the latter six consisted of 12 12.7mm Browning M2 machine guns, and they could also carry up to 1,360kg bombs in their internal bay. Operated by the CAEC's sole bomber squadron, they were left in their overall bare metal livery and served until replaced by more versatile Douglas B-26s in the late 1950s. (Artwork by Luca Canossa)

Between 1951 and 1958, the CAEC purchased a total of 11 de Havilland DHC-2 Beaver light liaison and transport aircraft. Early during their service with the CAEC, the Beavers were all left in a bare metal overall livery, as shown here. They saw heavy utilisation in counterinsurgency operations of the 1956-1958 period, when several were modified for combat operations. (Artwork by Tom Cooper)

The relatively small Cuban naval air service was established in 1935 and initially equipped with this de Havilland DH.60GM Moth. Delivered in silver dope overall, the aircraft received serial number 1 and was used as a primary trainer and for liaison duties. Later on, it was painted in olive green overall but retained its serial number and other markings. Notable are the black crossed anchors on the upper white field of the national marking on the rudder – the early symbol of Cuban naval aviation. (Artwork by Luca Canossa)

Through the late 1930s and early 1940s, Cuban naval aviation operated a miscellany of aircraft, including one Lockheed Sirius 8A (serial number 10), one Stinson SR-9D Reliant (serial number 51), three WACO UMF-3s, one Ford 4-AT Trimotor (serial number 53), and one Howard DGA-15W (serial number 54). In 1942, the Navy then received three Vought OS2U-3 Kingfishers. These remained in service until 1958 and were intensively used for counterinsurgency operations. On 10 November 1958, for example, Lieutenant Antonio E. Bascaró Sánches landed in rebel-controlled territory and was captured together with his aircraft. The rebels then repaired and used this Kingfisher in at least four combat sorties against the army. The OS2U-3s were armed with two M1919 machine guns and could carry up to 295kg of bombs. (Artwork by Luca Canossa)

Also in 1942, Cuban naval aviation received two Grumman JRF-5 Goose amphibians through the Lend-Lease program. They were used for transport purposes and flew coastal patrols. Like the Kingfishers, they were painted in the standard colours of the U.S. Navy for 1942, including NS Blue Gray on the top surfaces and sides and NS Light Gray on the lower surfaces. (Artwork by Luca Canossa)

Following a lengthy period without any new acquisitions, in 1956, Cuban naval aviation purchased seven Grumman TBM-3S2 Avenger torpedo bombers. They were operated as trainers and for coastal patrols but also saw deployment for counterinsurgency purposes before being assimilated into the FAR in 1959. Each was armed with two wing-mounted 12.7mm machine guns and one dorsal-mounted 12.7mm machine gun. Avengers could also carry up to 900kg of bombs in their weapons bay. As usual for ex-U.S. Navy aircraft of the early 1950s, they were painted in ANA 606 SG Sea Blue overall. (Artwork by Jean-Marie Guillou)

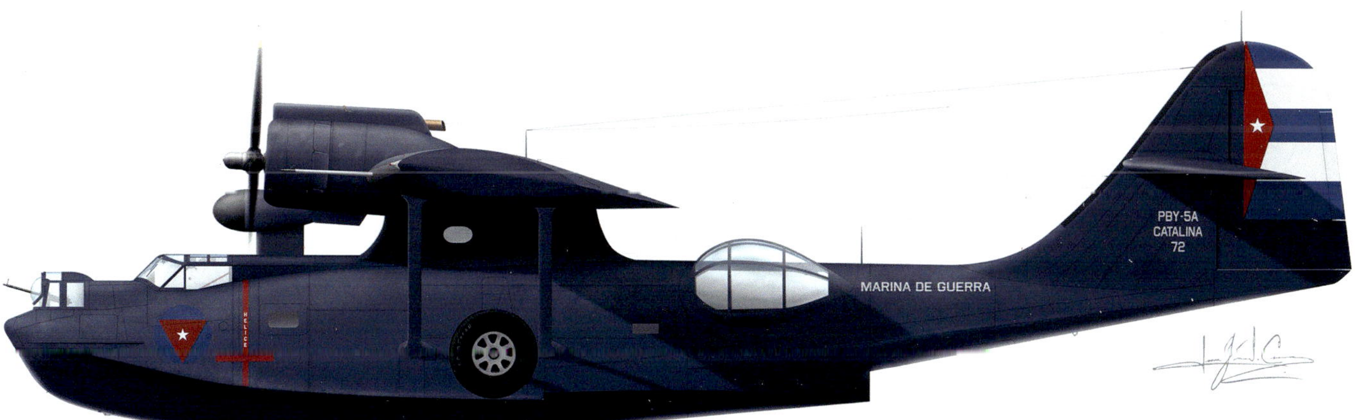

Except for three Curtiss SO3C Seamew patrol aircraft acquired from Great Britain in 1943, the last aircraft operated by Cuban naval aviation were six Consolidated OA-10 Catalinas, acquired in 1947, followed by two PBY-5As, purchased in 1950, and operated until 1958. All were painted in ANA 606 Sea Blue overall. They saw intensive deployment both for patrol duties and in counterinsurgency operations, for which they were armed with two 7.62mm machine guns in the front turret and two 12.7mm machine guns installed in waist blisters. Additionally, they could carry up to 1,800kg of bombs or depth charges. (Artwork by Luca Canossa)

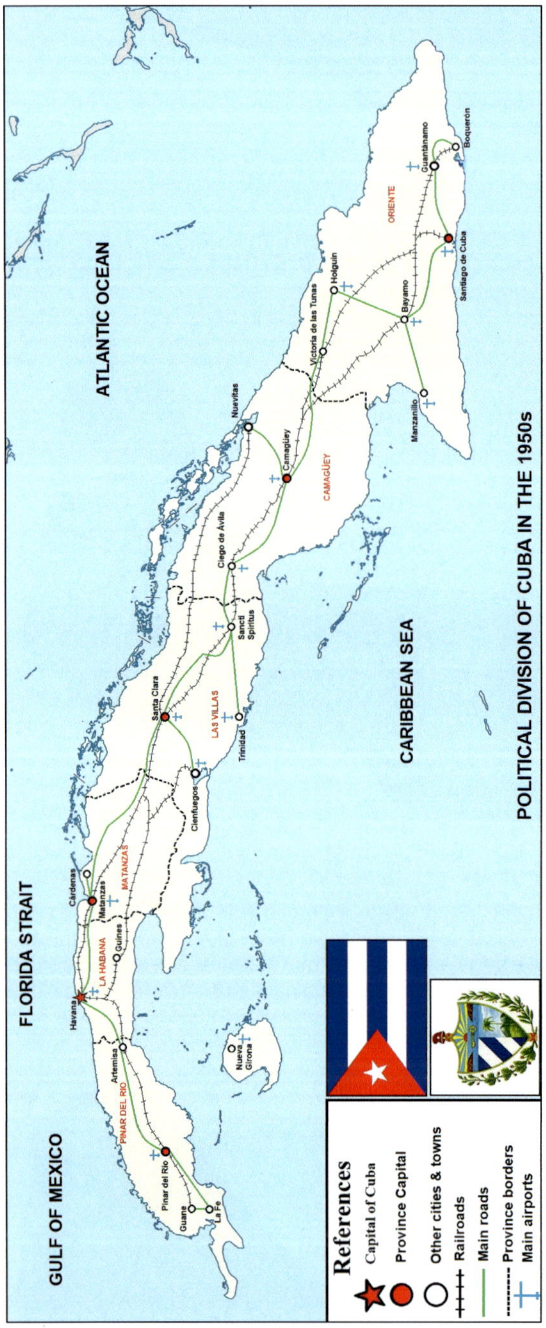

POLITICAL DIVISION OF CUBA IN THE 1950s

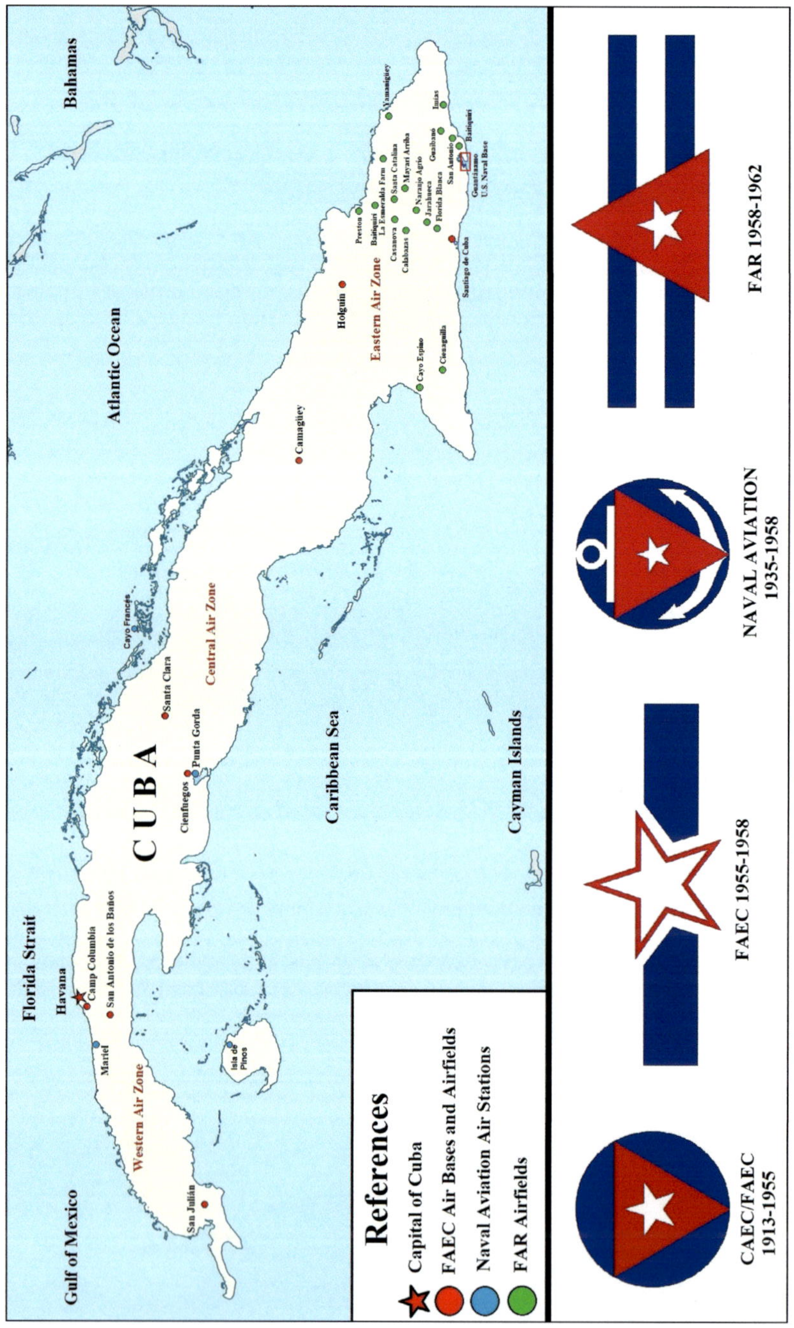

(Maps by Antonio Sapienza)

The coup d'état of 10 March 1952 made it possible for Batista to acquire the presidency of Cuba once again. The vast majority of the military supported him at that time. (Open source)

spots such as railways, radio stations, and government facilities were all occupied. President Carlos Prío, learning of the coup too late, tried to organise resistance but to no avail. He ended up seeking asylum in the Mexican Embassy.

Batista quickly reasserted himself, placing his old cronies back into positions of power. He publicly justified the takeover by claiming that President Prío had intended to stage his own coup in order to remain in power. The young firebrand lawyer Fidel Castro tried to bring Batista to court to answer for the illegal takeover, but he was thwarted; he thereupon decided that Batista could not be removed by legal means. Many Latin American countries quickly recognised the Batista government, and on 27 May the United States also extended formal recognition.

Upon seizing power, Batista inherited a country that was relatively prosperous by Latin American standards. According to Batista's government, although a third of Cubans still lived in poverty, Cuba was one of the five most developed countries in the region. In the 1950s, Cuba's gross domestic product (GDP) per capita was roughly equal to that of Italy at the time, although still only a sixth of that of the United States. Moreover, although corruption and inequality were rife under Batista, the wages of Cuba's industrial workers rose significantly. In 1953, the average Cuban family had an income of only $6.00 a week, 15% to 20% of the labour force was chronically unemployed, and only a third of the homes had running water. Despite this, according to the International Labour Organisation, the average industrial salary in Cuba had become the world's eighth-highest in 1958, and the average agricultural wage was higher than some European nations (although, according to one sample from 1956 to 1957, agricultural workers could only find employment for an average of 123 days per year while farm owners, rural tenants and sharecroppers worked an average of only 135 days per year).

Lucrative business in Batista's Cuba

The Batista era was a golden age of tourism in Cuba. Americans flocked to the island for relaxation and to stay at the famous hotels and gamble at the casinos. The American mafia had a strong presence in Havana, and Lucky Luciano lived there for a time. Legendary mobster Meyer Lansky worked with Batista to complete

President Carlos Prio Socarras (1948-1952) (left), deposed by Fulgencio Batista (1952-1959) (right). (Open source)

projects, including the Havana Riviera Hotel. Batista took a huge cut of all casino takings and amassed millions. Famous celebrities liked to visit, and Cuba became synonymous with a good time for vacationers. Acts headlined by celebrities such as Ginger Rogers and Frank Sinatra performed at the hotels. Even American Vice President Richard Nixon visited the country.

It was not just hotels and casinos since brothels also flourished. A major industry grew up around them as government officials received bribes and policemen collected protection money. Prostitutes could be seen standing in doorways, strolling the streets, or leaning from windows. One report estimated that 11,500 of them plied their trade in Havana. Beyond the outskirts of the capital, beyond the slot machines, one of the most beautiful countries in the Western world was juxtaposed with one of the poorest. Throughout the 1950s, Havana served as 'a hedonistic playground for the world's elite', producing sizable gambling, prostitution and drug profits for the American mafia, corrupt law-enforcement officials, and their politically elected cronies. As stated before, in a bid to profit from such an environment, Batista established lasting relationships with organised crime, notably with the American mobsters Meyer Lansky and Lucky Luciano, and under his rule, Havana became known as 'the Latin Las Vegas'. Batista and Lansky formed a friendship and

The opulent lifestyle in cities like Havana and Varadero was mostly for American tourists and upper- and middle-class Cubans in the 1950s. The poverty in the county's interior, however, remained impressive. (Open source)

business relationship that flourished for a decade. During a stay at the Waldorf-Astoria in New York in the late 1940s, it was mutually agreed that, in return for kickbacks, Batista would give Lansky and the Mafia control of Havana's racetracks and casinos. After World War II, Luciano was paroled from prison on the condition that he return permanently to Sicily. Luciano secretly moved to Cuba, where he worked to resume control over American Mafia operations. Luciano also ran a number of casinos in Cuba with the sanction of Batista, though the American government eventually succeeded in pressuring the Batista government to deport him.

Brothers Fidel and Raúl Castro in the early 1950s. They would later lead a revolution that ultimately overthrew the Batista regime in 1959. (Open source)

Batista encouraged large-scale gambling in Havana. In 1955, he announced that Cuba would grant a gaming licence to anyone who invested US$1 million in a hotel or $200,000 in a new nightclub and that the government would provide matching public funds for construction, a 10-year tax exemption, and waive duties on imported equipment and furnishings for new hotels. Each casino would pay the government US$250,000 for the licence, plus a percentage of the profits. As the new hotels, nightclubs, and casinos opened, Batista collected his share of the profits. His wife's 'bagman' collected 10% of the profits nightly at Santo Trafficante's casinos, the Sans Souci cabaret, and the casinos in the hotels Sevilla-Biltmore, Commodoro, Deauville, and Capri. His take from the Lansky casinos, his prized Habana Riviera, the Hotel Nacional, the Montmartre Club, and others was said to be 30%. Lansky was said to have personally contributed millions of dollars per year to Batista's Swiss bank accounts.

Fidel Castro and revolution

Castro, who would likely have been elected to Congress had the elections taken place, had learned that there was no way of legally removing Batista and began organising a revolution. On 26 July 1953, brothers Fidel and Raul Castro and 165 rebels attacked the army barracks at Moncada in Santiago de Cuba, igniting the Cuban Revolution. The attack failed and the Castro brothers were jailed, but it brought them a great deal of attention. Many captured rebels were executed on the spot, resulting in a lot of negative press for the government. In prison, Fidel Castro began organising the 26th of July Movement (M-26-7), named after the date of the Moncada assault.

Batista had been aware of Castro's rising political star for some time and had once even given Castro a $1,000 wedding present in an attempt to keep him friendly. After Moncada, Castro went to jail, but not before publicly turning his own trial into criticism of Batista's illegal power grab. In the 1954 elections, Batista was the only candidate, and upon being elected, he reaffirmed his authoritarian government. In 1955 Batista ordered the release of many political prisoners, including those who had attacked Moncada. The Castro brothers thereupon went to Mexico to organise the revolution.

President Batista and the American pilot Leo Povey had a long friendship (left). 'Tell me who you hang out with, and I'll tell you who you are' (popular proverb): Fulgencio Batista encouraged the installation of casinos in Cuba, forming partnerships with notorious gangsters and mafiosi like Meyer Lansky (right). (P.R.B.J. Collection)

The seed for a future revolution had been planted. Outside of the splendour and nightlife in Havana, things were grim. Poor Cubans saw little benefit from the tourism boom, and more and more of them tuned into rebel radio broadcasts. As the rebels in the mountains gained strength and influence, Batista's police and security forces turned increasingly to torture and murder in an effort to root out the rebellion.

By late 1955, student riots and anti-Batista demonstrations had become frequent, and unemployment became a problem as graduates entering the workforce could not find jobs. These were dealt with through increasing repression. All youth were seen as suspected revolutionaries. Due to its continued opposition to Batista and the large amount of revolutionary activity taking place on its campus, the University of Havana was temporarily closed on 30 November 1956, and it was not reopened until 1959 under the revolutionary government.

In April 1956, Batista called popular military leader Col. Ramón Barquín back to Cuba from his post as military attaché to the United States. Believing Barquín would support his rule, Batista promoted him to general. Barquín's *Conspiración de los Puros* (Conspiracy of the Pure), however, was already underway and had already progressed too far. On 6 April 1956, Barquín led hundreds of career officers in a coup attempt but was frustrated by Lieutenant Ríos Morejón, who betrayed the plan. Barquín was sentenced to solitary confinement for eight years on the Isle of Pines, while some officers were sentenced to death for treason. Many others, however, were allowed to remain in the military without reprimand. The purge of the officer corps contributed to the inability of the Cuban Army to successfully combat Castro later on, as the military leaders loyal to Batista were deeply inept.

On 13 March 1957, student leader José Antonio Echeverría was killed by police outside *Radio Reloj* in Havana after announcing that Batista had been killed in a student attack on the Presidential Palace. In reality, Batista survived, and the students of the Federation of University Students (FEU) and the *Directorio Revolucionario* (DR) who led the attack were killed in the response carried out by the military and police. Castro quickly condemned the attack since the 26 July Movement (M-26-7) had not participated in it.

Exit from power

In Mexico, the Castro brothers found many disillusioned Cubans willing to fight for the revolution. They also picked up Argentine doctor Ernesto 'Che' Guevara. In November 1956, they returned to Cuba on board the yacht *Granma*. For a couple of years, they waged a guerrilla war against Batista. The M-26-7 was joined by others inside Cuba who did their part to destabilise the nation, including the Revolutionary Directorate, the student group that Batista had alienated years before, which almost assassinated him in March 1957.

By 1958, Castro and his men controlled huge sections of the country and had their own hospital, schools and radio stations. Elections were scheduled for June, as required by the Constitution, but were delayed until November, when Castro and the revolutionaries called for a general strike and placed several bombs in civilian areas of the country. Three main candidates ran in the elections: Carlos Márquez Sterling of the Party of the Free People, former President Ramón Grau San Martín of the Cuban Revolutionary Party-Authentic, and Andrés Rivero Agüero of the government coalition. Fraud occurred during these elections, and Batista made sure his candidate, Rivero Agüero, would 'win', although he would never assume the presidency.

By late 1958, it was clear that the Cuban Revolution would win, and when 'Che' Guevara's column captured the city of Santa Clara, Batista decided it was time to go. On 31 December 1958, he authorised some of his officers to deal with the rebels, letting them know that he was leaving the country. In the early hours of 1 January 1959, Batista, his wife and his children fled to Santo Domingo, Dominican Republic, by plane, together with high officials of his government, allegedly taking millions of dollars with them. Some sources claim he took some US$300 million that he had amassed through graft and payoffs!

Death

The wealthy exiled president never returned to politics, even though he was still only in his 50s when he fled Cuba. He eventually settled in Portugal, first in Madeira and later in Estoril, and worked for an insurance company. He also wrote six books between 1939 and 1964 and died on 6 August 1973, in Marbella, Spain.

Legacy

Batista was corrupt, violent and out of touch with his people (or perhaps he simply didn't care about them). Still, in comparison with some of his fellow dictators, such as the Somozas in Nicaragua, Trujillo in the Dominican Republic or the Duvaliers in Haiti, he was relatively benign. Much of his money was made by taking bribes and payoffs from foreigners, such as his percentage from the haul

President Batista met his American counterpart, Eisenhower, for the last time in 1956. Two years later, Eisenhower would withdraw all his support and impose an arms embargo on Batista's government for having used American combat aircraft against the rebels in Cayo Loco, Cienfuegos, in 1957 (left). Batista with Vice President Richard Nixon in 1956 (right). (Rogali collection)

The main leaders of the 26 July Movement (M-26-7): From left to right, Fidel and Raúl Castro, 'Che' Guevara and Camilo Cienfuegos. (Open source)

President-elect Andrés Rivero Agüero (centre) in the fraudulent elections of 3 November 1958. Agüero was Batista's puppet candidate but would never assume the presidency since Castro's revolutionary forces took power on 1 January 1959. (Open source)

from the casinos. Therefore, he looted state funds less than other dictators did. He frequently ordered the murder of prominent political rivals, but ordinary Cubans had little to fear from him until the revolution began, when his tactics turned increasingly brutal and repressive.

The Cuban Revolution was less the result of Batista's cruelty, corruption, and indifference than it was of Fidel Castro's ambition. Castro's charisma, conviction, and ambition were singular: he would have clawed his way to the top or died trying. Batista was in Castro's way, so he removed him.

That's not to say that Batista did not help Castro greatly. At the time of the revolution, most Cubans despised Batista, the exceptions being the very wealthy who were sharing in the loot. Had he shared Cuba's new wealth with his people, organised a return to democracy and improved living conditions for the poorest Cubans, Castro's revolution might never have taken hold. Even Cubans who have fled Castro's Cuba and constantly rail against him rarely defend Batista; perhaps the only thing they agree on with Castro is that Batista had to go.

Castro and his henchmen defeated a six-year corrupt right-wing dictatorship and established a communist regime that has survived for more than 65 years to date. Fidel Castro was first prime minister between 1959 and 1976, with absolute control of the armed forces. Then, between 1976 and 2008, he was president of the Council of State, being replaced by his brother Raúl. Fidel Castro died in Havana at the age of 90 on 25 November 2016.

After a futile military campaign against the guerrillas, President Batista decided to flee Cuba with his family and senior collaborators of his government in the early morning hours of 1 January 1959. (Open source)

Fulgencio Batista and his family during his golden exile, on the right, in Spain, where he took up residence and died in 1973, and on the left during a trip to Portugal in the 1960s. (Open source)

5

THE CARIBBEAN LEGION IN CAYO CONFITES

The *Legión del Caribe* (Caribbean Legion) was a group of Latin American leaders, exiles, and revolutionaries in the 1940s who had the aim of overthrowing dictatorships across Central America and replacing them with democratic governments. The members of the legion came from most of the countries in Latin America, although the largest number was from the Dominican Republic. The stated targets of the legion were the dictatorships of Rafael Trujillo in the Dominican Republic and Teodoro Picado in Costa Rica. The legion was responsible for two failed invasions of the Dominican Republic, in 1947 and 1949, as well as for successfully toppling the Costa Rican government in the Costa Rican Civil War in 1948.

The activities of the Caribbean Legion began in 1946 after the end of World War II. The emergence of democracy in Cuba, Venezuela and Guatemala during the previous few years resulted in pro-democracy activists in other countries becoming more ambitious. The dictatorships of Rafael Trujillo in the Dominican Republic and Anastasio Somoza García in Nicaragua were seen as particularly tyrannical and thus became targets of the legion.

In the summer of 1947, a group of approximately 1,500 armed men, mainly Cubans and Dominicans, was assembled in Cuba with the covert assistance of Cuban President Ramón Grau San Martín. The military leaders of the group were former Dominican General Juan Rodríguez (chief), Rolando Masferrer, Eufemio Fernández, Feliciano Maderne and Jorge Rivas. They believed that with their own strength and the assistance of the Dominican underground, they would be able to overthrow the US-backed dictator Rafael Trujillo. The preparations of the force were not kept very secret, and its intent was very public.

The Cayo Confites expedition in particular was a military movement against the government of Rafael Leonidas Trujillo in

Some of the leaders of the Caribbean Legion on the Cayo Confites Expedition: General Juan 'Juancito' Rodríguez, with beret and light shirt (top left); Juan Bosch (top right); Fidel Castro and others aboard the LCI *El Fantasma* (bottom left); and from left to right, Commander Guillermo Genaris, Lieutenant Colonel Rolando Masferrer, Dr Rafael Mainardi and Lieutenant Colonel Eufemio Fernández (bottom right). (Open source & Cubadebate.org)

the Dominican Republic that promoted the armed invasion to overthrow the regime. Its name came from the key belonging to the Camagüey archipelago, located in the Atlantic Ocean, called Cayo Confites, located some 350 aerial miles northwest of Ciudad Trujillo (now Santo Domingo), the capital of the Dominican Republic. The decision to organise an armed expedition was approved by Dominican political exiles when it was evident that a democratic transition would not take place through peaceful means in their country.

By early 1947, in the midst of the democratic atmosphere after the Second World War, Rafael Leónidas Trujillo found himself surrounded by governments opposed to his regime: Rómulo Betancourt in Venezuela, Juan José Arévalo in Guatemala, Ramón Grau San Martín in Cuba and Elie Lescot in Haiti.

By April 1947, the leaders of the invasion had managed to accumulate a large amount of weapons in addition to gathering together some 500 Dominican volunteer combatants. By the following month, the force had reached 1,500 troops, having been augmented with Cuban volunteers and other nationalities, some of them veterans of the Spanish Civil War and World War II. The leaders established their headquarters and base of operations at the San Luis Hotel in Havana.

On 13 July 1947, the exiles elected a central committee to direct the expedition made up of the former Dominican general Juan Rodríguez García, aka 'Juancito', Ángel Morales, Leovigildo Cuello, Juan Bosch and Juan Isidro Jiménez Grullón. Days later, the expedition members left Havana for the Holguín Polytechnic in eastern Cuba, where they received military training under the orders of Manolo Bordas, who held the rank of lieutenant in the U.S. Army and who organised the expedition members into four battalions:

- **Sandino Battalion:** Its commander was Rolando Masferrer, a Cuban lawyer and veteran of the Spanish Civil War. He served as military leader of the expedition.
- **Guiteras Battalion:** Its commander was Eufemio Fernández, a Cuban doctor and another veteran of the Spanish Civil War.
- **Luperón Battalion:** Its commander was Jorge Rivas Monte, a Honduran career officer and military graduate of the Guatemalan Military School.
- **Máximo Gómez Battalion:** Its commander was Feliciano Maderne, another career officer and military leader of the Gibara expedition.

From the Holguín polytechnic, the expedition members were transferred to Nipe Bay, where the ship *Aurora* and the schooner *Berta* were waiting for them with a large part of the cargo for the expedition. They then boarded the boats and headed towards Cayo Confites. In the midst of military exercises, landing practices and other manoeuvres, the expedition effectives expected to count on more ships, as well as a good number of aircraft for solid air support. At the beginning of September, the movement had seven ships, 24 planes and 1,200 armed men. Among the expedition members were José Horacio Rodríguez, Ramón Emilio Mejía, Mauricio Báez, Miguel Ángel Ramírez Alcántara, Fidel Castro, Carlos Gutiérrez Menoyo, Humberto Castelló Aldanás, Pedro Mir, Francisco Alberto Horacio Vázquez, Federico Horacio Vázquez, Germán Martínez Reyna, Nicanor Saleta Arias, Miguel Ángel Feliú Arseno, Horacio Julio Ornes Coiscou, José Rolando Martínez Bonilla, Ángel Miolán, Freddy Fernández Barreiro, Pagán Perdomo Data, the brothers Víctor, Rafael and Virgilio Mainardi Reyna and Antonio Toirac Escasena.

Juan Bosch made extensive efforts to find military aircraft on the United States surplus market, something they had to do discreetly as they were aware that American legislation was strict regarding the export of military equipment. The acquisition of military aircraft by irregular means was not uncommon at the time since many Latin American countries were headed by dictators whose governments, although supported by the United States, were not looked upon favourably and were thus unable to obtain approval for the acquisition of combat aircraft. The megalomaniacal desire of

Generalissimo Rafael Leónidas Trujillo (1891-1961) was the president of the Dominican Republic first between 1930 and 1938 and then between 1942 and 1952. (Open source)

On the left, two of the expeditionary ships, the LCI No. 1006, known as *El Fantasma* (The Phantom), and the LCT *Aurora*, in Cayo Confites in 1947. On the right, expeditionary troops preparing for the invasion of the Dominican Republic. (*Bohemia* Magazine)

some of these dictators in pursuit of purchasing military equipment favoured the emergence of a very profitable market for arms dealers selling combat aircraft, among other things. In the post-war era, there was an abundance of surplus aircraft obtainable at high prices, although in various degrees of preservation and often devoid of spare parts, which could be smuggled into the purchasing country.

In the case of the Caribbean Legion revolutionaries, it was no different; they were able to find 'specialist' traders who acquired a myriad of planes, the vast majority of which were of questionable usefulness. One such trader was Reinaldo Rosell, located at Bush Field in Georgia, who consulted Hugh Baron of the US War Assets Administration (WAA) on the criteria and conditions of licenses for the acquisition of surplus aircraft. Since Baron realised that Rosell had very limited knowledge on the subject, he recommended the hiring of William Moye, who actively participated in the acquisition and operation of aircraft for the *Legion del Caribe*.

To support the exile militia, a veritable fleet of planes was acquired, most likely organised by José Horácio Rodriguez. To conceal the operation, an airline was created, *Aerovias Cubana-Norte Americanas* (Cuban-North American Airways, ACNA), which began operations with a Douglas C-47 with the American registration number NC56001. William Moye was its main pilot,

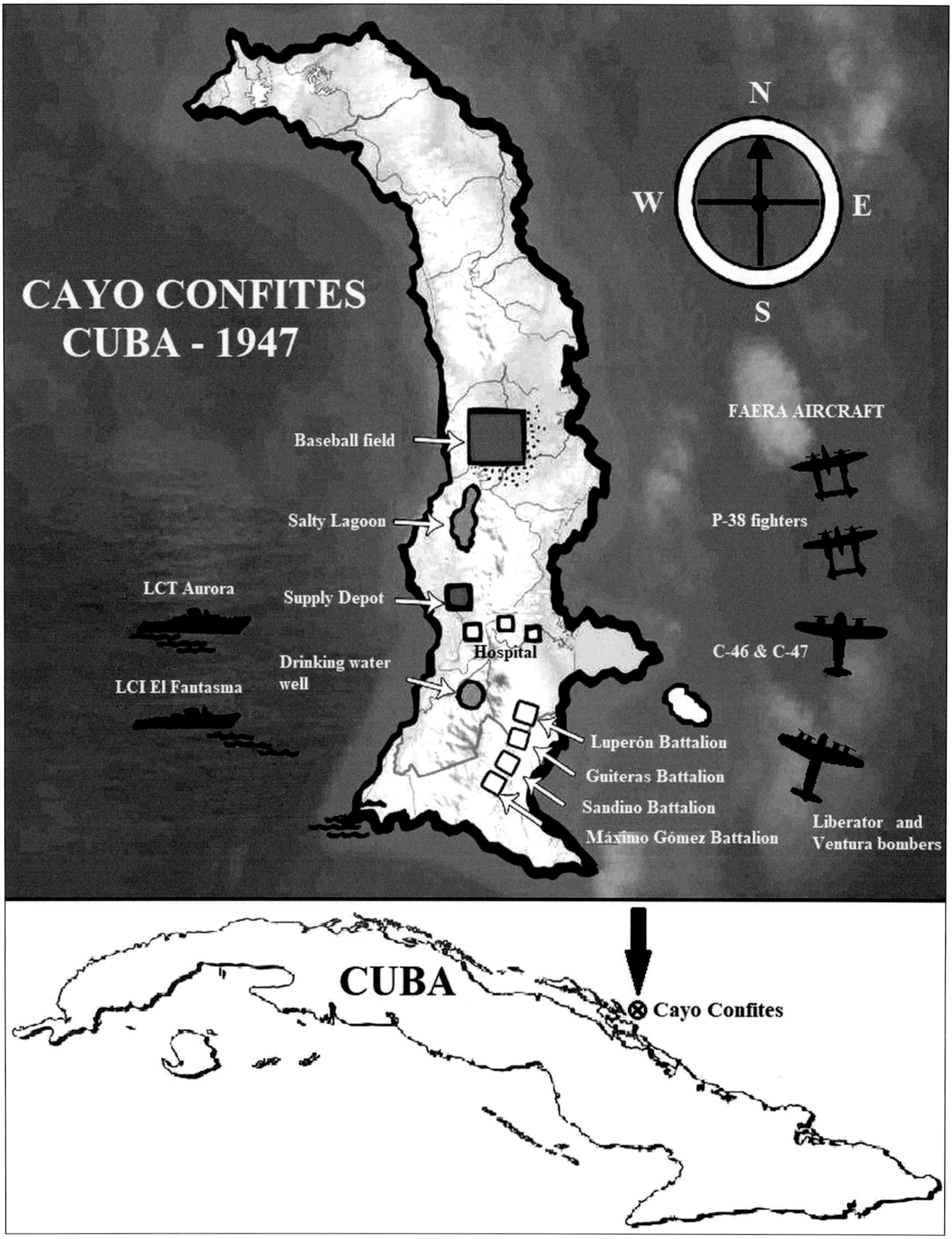

Deployment of the expeditionary force at Cayo Confites, Cuba. (Authors)

A Consolidated PB4Y-1 that was seized by US authorities in Ponca City, Oklahoma, bound for Cuba (top) (UP Wirephoto). A Douglas C-47DL, registration number CU-T263, belonging to *Aerovías Cubanas Internacionales* (ACNA), expressly acquired to support the Dominican Revolutionary Movement (bottom). (George Farinas)

An *Aerovías Cubanas Internacionales* Douglas DC-4, registration number NC44567, at Rancho Boyeros airport in Havana, Cuba, in June 1946, with the name *La Ruta de Colón* (Columbus Route) painted on the fuselage. What is interesting in this picture are the rows of Cuban naval aviation aircraft in the background, including Curtiss Seamews, Vought Kingfishers, Ford 4-AT Trimotors and Grumman Gooses, as well as other aircraft. (Reinaldo Ramirez-Rosell)

and it made several flights connecting Florida and Georgia with Cuba. Later, another C-47 was purchased, also with an American registration number – NC66113.

The planes operated out of the Rancho Boyeros airport, and although it was blatantly obvious they were being used to supply the revolutionaries, the Cuban government made no attempt to interfere since they had mutual interests, that of invading and overthrowing disaffected governments in neighbouring countries. There is an unfounded claim that the rebel invasion was to have been supported by paratroopers transported in CAEC aircraft, but no documents have been found supporting this.

In addition to the two C-47s, the fleet was bolstered by at least one Cessna T-50 Bobcat and two Vultee BT-13 primary trainers, which remained with the *Academia Nacional de Aviación-Reserva Aérea-CAEC* (National Aviation Academy-Air Reserve, ANACRA) in Rancho Boyeros. The BT-13s served as instruction aircraft for pilots of unknown origin trained by American instructor Kenneth Robinson. Of the two BT-13s, one crashed, and the other was taken back to the United States piloted by Kenneth Robinson himself.

William Moye was the intermediary in the acquisition of three Lockheed B-34 Ventura twin-engine aircraft (USAAF registration numbers 41-38020, 41-38032 and 41-38082). The three planes were originally at Bush Field, Georgia, and one of them, B-34 41-3802, was detained en route to Cuba by American customs agents in Key West, Florida, in autumn 1945, as it lacked the requisite export documents. As for the two other B-34s, 41-38082 was lost shortly after takeoff, killing the pilot in January 1947. In July that same year, the third B-34 was flown to Cuba, piloted by Chester H. Pickup, and in the following month, the B-34 that had been detained in Key West finally managed to reach Cuba – also having been piloted by Pickup.

At the same time, Pickup was engaged in checking out some surplus Consolidated Liberator four-engine bombers that were being made available for scrap at a cost of just US$1,000 each. Through consultation with Hugh Baron, a PB4Y-1 (the naval version of the B-24 Liberator four-engine bomber) was purchased together with a Curtiss C-46 for a total value of US$10,000 in the name of an intermediary called Karl Knight. At the same time, Rosell also acquired a Grumman J2F-6 Duck seaplane (U.S. Navy registration BuA 32712) for US$1,000. On 30 July 1947, the Liberator PB4Y-1 departed from Bush Field towards Cuba piloted by Pickup but returned shortly afterwards due to mechanical problems. The following day, however, it landed at Rancho Boyeros loaded with military equipment for the rebels.

Aiming to increase the fleet of Liberators, two more aircraft were purchased (a PB4Y-1 and a B-24L); however, both were detained and seized by American authorities, one of them in Ponca City, Oklahoma, on 6 November, and the other in Tulsa, Oklahoma, the next day. Nevertheless, the idea of having a fleet of bombers continued with the acquisition of twin-engine North American B-25 Mitchells. Two of them, a B-25C (ex-USAAF serial number 42-32385) and a B-25H (ex-USAAF serial number 43-4536), were acquired through Universal Aviation Co. in Tulsa, Oklahoma. They managed to be delivered to Cuba; however, the initial plan of acquiring eight planes was thwarted when a third aircraft purchased from the same company was detained and confiscated in Tulsa. Complementing the bombers, two Douglas B-18 Bolos were also acquired, but little is known about the operation of these aircraft.

In addition to the bombers mentioned, six P-38 Lightning fighters were also purchased, all of which were originally P-38Ls. Three of the aircraft, however, had been converted to the P-38M night fighter version with added space for a second occupant who would serve as the radar operator, even though these particular aircraft did not have radars. All of these aircraft had little flying time since they had been accepted into the USAAF between May and June 1945. Moreover, all of them had been obtained in a murky and clandestine way. Two of them came via Universal Aviation Co., while two others came via Charles Babb Co. of Kingman, Arizona, a well-known company selling war surplus planes. The P-38s arrived in Cuba, landing at Camp Columbia and in Mariel; however, when the last of the six aircraft landed at Camp Columbia on 23 August 1947, it was seized by the Cuban authorities, as the political situation regarding the admission of rebels into Cuban territory had changed. So the P-38s were never actually in the hands of the expeditionaries.

The insurgents also had to wait for their aircraft to be equipped with weapons. The aircraft squadron by this time included P-38L/M Lightning fighters, a PB4Y-1 Liberator heavy bomber, B-34 Ventura patrol bombers, B-25C/H Mitchell medium bombers, B-18 Bolo bombers, BT-13A Valiant basic trainers, and C-46, C-47, C-54, C-60 Lodestar, and UC-78 Bobcat transport aircraft. These aircraft were mostly based at the Rancho Boyeros airport near Havana in Cuba, with some others parked at Mariel Naval Air Base since Cayo Confites lacked adequate infrastructure. It was reported some of them were even deployed at the Antonio Maceo airport in Santiago de Cuba. Additionally, a J2F-6 Duck utility amphibian, a PB4Y-1 Privateer and a B-24 Liberator heavy bomber were confiscated in Miami, Ponca City and Tulsa, respectively, before flying to Cuba. There were plans to acquire at least another 6 C-47s, but their purchase was never finalised.

With this fleet of aircraft, what was pompously called the *Fuerza Aérea del Ejército de la Revolución Americana* (Air Force of the American Revolution Army, FAERA) – a subordinate element of the Dominican Revolutionary Movement – was formed, at least on paper. Most of the aircraft were to be flown by mercenary pilots commanded by the American Louis C. Dell, who claimed to be a former World War II veteran of the 'Flying Tigers'. Other Americans included the aforementioned Karl Knight and Chester H. Pickup, both assigned to the heavy bombers. In fact, the latter two American pilots were the ones who acquired the PB4Y-1 bomber from the War Assets Administration in the US. The list also included Frank Adkins, Luis M. Bordas, Frank D. Oreal, Arthur Roscoe, Frank O'Neal and John Alexander, who were in charge of the ferry flights of the P-38 Lightning fighters to Cuba on 27 August 1947. In total, between pilots and ground crews (mechanics), there were approximately 30 American mercenaries, mostly World War II veterans.

All the FAERA aircraft would eventually be confiscated by the Cuban Army Air Corps and flown to Camp Columbia by Cuban pilots. They soon received CAEC serials and markings, with the exception of 1 C-46, 1 C-47, and the two UC-78s. These transport aircraft were operated by *Aerovías Cubana-Norte Americanas* (ACNA), which had its main offices in Havana. Its president was Reinaldo R. Rosell, the trader who had consulted Hugh Baron of the U.S. War Assets Administration about surplus aircraft, and one of its pilots was the American Robert L. Brown. The sole purpose of the ACNA was to support the Dominican Revolutionary Movement.

None of the illegal flight deliveries of FAERA aircraft would have been possible without the overt assistance of high-ranking Cuban authorities, especially the minister of education, and even the Cuban Navy and Naval Air Force, which provided 100-octane aviation fuel from its own stockpile.

FAERA aircraft did not carry any identification markings, and their previous American emblems, serials and registrations had been crudely painted over.

Table 2: FAERA aircraft types[1]

Aircraft	No. of aircraft	Role	Fate
Lockheed P-38L Lightning	3	Fighter	Seized by the CAEC in Cuba
Lockheed P-38M Lightning	3	Night fighter	Seized by the CAEC in Cuba
Consolidated PB4Y-1 Liberator	2	Heavy bomber	One seized by the CAEC in Cuba and the other by the US government in Ponca City, OK.
Consolidated B-24 Liberator	1	Heavy bomber	Seized by the US government in Tulsa, OK.
Lockheed B-34 Ventura	3	Patrol bomber	Two seized by the CAEC in Cuba One crashed in Augusta-Galveston
North American B-25C/H Mitchell	1/1	Medium bomber	Seized by the CAEC in Cuba
North American B-25 Mitchell (Sub type unknown)	1	Medium bomber	Seized by American Customs in Tulsa, OK.
Douglas RB-18A Bolo	1	Medium bomber	Registered in Costa Rica as TI-205, the aircraft was flown to Guatemala to join the FAERA. It was later sold in Jamaica under registration number NC1037M.
Vultee BT-13A Valiant	2	Basic trainer	One crashed in Cuba during pilot training and the other returned to the US flown by an American pilot.
Grumman J2F-6 Duck	1	Utility amphibian	Seized by the US government in Miami, FL.
Curtiss C-46 Commando	1	Transport	Seized by the CAEC in Cuba
Douglas C-47	3	Transport	Seized by the CAEC in Cuba
Lockheed C-60A Lodestar	1	Transport	Crashed on 12 April 1948 at Zacapa, Guatemala
Cessna UC-78 Bobcat	2	Light transport	Seized in Cuba

Note: A Consolidated PBY-5A Catalina was also seized but it was not related to FAERA. This PBY had a French crew and it was transferred to the CAEC first and ended up in the Cuban Naval Air Force later.

Some of the FAERA aircraft confiscated by the CAEC after the failed Cayo Confites expedition. A Consolidated PB4Y-1 Liberator (top left), a Lockheed P-38M NC67849 with a North American B-25H Mitchell in the background (top right), one of three Lockheed B-34 Venturas (bottom left), and another P-38M (bottom right). (History of Cuban Military Aviation/HAMC and Memoria del Ministerio de Guerra y Marina)

The legion had seven ships for transporting troops:

- LCT *Libertad*, renamed *Aurora*.
- LCI No.1006, renamed *El Fantasma* (The Phantom) and later *Máximo Gómez*.
- The Dominican armoured schooner *Angelita*, designated *Maceo*.
- The emergency rescue boat *Victoria*, called *Berta*, had already been seized.
- An LCI renamed *Patria*, which had been held in Baltimore in August 1947.
- Two PT boats used in World War II, stationed at the Mariel base.

All these ships, except for the LCI *Patria*, were seized by the Cuban Navy.

On 13 July 1947, a central committee was elected to direct the expedition against Trujillo. It was in precisely that same month that the US government, upon learning of the invasion plans, began to pressure President Grau San Martín to stop the military action that was being prepared against Trujillo. To this end, the US ambassador in Havana, Henry Norweb, met twice each with both President Grau and his foreign minister. Meanwhile, the Cuban president sought support from the Haitian government of Elie Lescot so that both the naval landing and a land invasion could be carried out through Haitian territory, in addition to providing a safe space where weapons and ammunition could be stored. Elie Lescot, in addition to agreeing to these requests, contributed US$25,000 to the expedition.

On 22 July 1947, Trujillo learned that the Cuban government was involved in supporting an invasion of the Dominican Republic, compelling him to launch a series of protests against Cuba through diplomatic channels. Weeks later, faced with the imminent departure of the expedition members, Trujillo sent a message to Cuban President Grau San Martín warning him that the moment the expedition members set foot on Dominican territory, both Havana and Santiago de Cuba would be bombed by the Dominican Air Force and he would declare war on Cuba.

President Trujillo sought the backing of the militarist regimes of Brazil and Argentina, which provided him with decisive hemispheric support. Meanwhile, the Trujillo government's political propaganda regarding the danger of the country falling into communist hands prompted the United States to lift its arms embargo on the Dominican Republic, reaching a new agreement with the prevailing regime. Trujillo, presuming American support, arrested and even massacred the socialist and communist leaders of his country.

Trujillo had already directed enormous efforts to destabilise those governments that were sheltering Dominican exiles by engaging in plots of all kinds, ranging from the co-optation and bribery of journalists to supporting coup attempts and terrorist attacks. The Cuban democratic government of President Grau San Martín had already been a victim of these Machiavellian plans on Trujillo's part, and for that reason his administration offered significant logistical support to the Dominican exiles who had opted for an armed struggle. It was from this that the plan for what would later be known as the Cayo Confites expedition emerged. The governments of Juan José Arévalo of Guatemala and Rómulo Betancourt in Venezuela also joined in this operation to support the Caribbean revolutionary adventure. Arévalo provided the light weapons while Betancourt was in charge of providing air support for the landing. By 1947, however, international conditions had changed abruptly, and with the beginning of Cold War policy, the United States began supporting the right-wing dictatorial regimes of Latin America in every way.

It was then that the Cuban government, under intense pressure from the United States, decided to move the expedition members to the more secluded Cayo Confites, some 350 aerial miles northwest of Ciudad Trujillo. As Cuban Navy Captain Carlos M. Alfonso, commander of the naval base at La Fé on Cuba's southwest coast, would later recall, one day he received a sudden visit from Naval Ensign Alberto Juarrero, who, piloting a Vought OS2U Kingfisher floatplane, brought a message ordering Captain Alfonso to assume command of the patrol vessel GC-101 *Leoncio Prado*. Captain Alfonso, accompanied by two other officers – Escanel and Cansio – reported to naval headquarters, where he was told to take the night train to the port of Antilla in Cuba's western Holguín Province. When they arrived at the port, the GC-101, which had formerly been under the command of Ensign Andrés González Lines, was already awaiting them.

Once boarded, the GC-101 headed across Nipe Bay to Preston (now Guatemala), where they loaded up with supplies and drinking water. Upon leaving Preston, the coast guard observed the presence of an armed LCI, which – upon being detected – immediately turned about and began to flee. This was immediately reported to headquarters, but an encrypted message gave the patrol vessel clear instructions 'neither to pursue nor to harass [the LCI] but to render it all assistance as required'. Following the route of the LCI, they eventually reached the Central Preston roadstead, where, upon docking, they discovered there were more than a thousand armed men under the command of General Rodríguez and Captain Feliciano Maderne. The GC-101 eventually escorted the expedition members to Cayo Confites, but the planned expedition soon fell apart.

By moving the expedition forces to a different, more secluded spot, President Grau intended to wash his hands of Washington and not be compromised by the support he had been giving to the Dominican exiles. This relocation caused alarm in both the United States and the Dominican Republic, as it was believed that the invasion had begun. Days passed, and nothing more was heard about the supposed invaders until 11 August of that year, when reconnaissance planes from the U.S. Navy located the insurgents in the Cayo Confites area. Knowledge about the force's new location was made possible by information provided by British deserters who fled from Cayo Confites. Another problem for the invading force was the antagonism between the different internal groups, which did not get along politically, mainly between the Cubans and the Dominicans, so it can be said that the legion was not a cohesive force. One of the Cubans who would later achieve notoriety in his own country was Fidel Castro. There was also enormous tension at this moment between President Grau San Martín, who had sponsored, authorised, and helped organise the expedition, and General Genovevo Pérez Dámera, chief of staff of the Cuban Army, who had been sidelined.

At the same time, Grau also intended to gain time and ensure the most appropriate moment for either the expedition's departure or its definitive dissolution. Meanwhile, President Truman's administration was doing everything possible to dismantle the expedition of Dominican exiles who were on Cuban soil. Among these actions, it is worth highlighting the invitation to Washington made to the aforementioned General Pérez Dámera to discuss the issue of Cayo Confites. Perhaps unsurprisingly, upon his return to Cuba, the Cuban Army 'discovered' a large arsenal of weapons belonging to the Dominican exiles. At the same time, the clandestine sale of weapons on American soil to these same exiles was pursued and halted, while measures were taken to ensure that Trujillo's armed forces had 'enough' not only to maintain internal order in the Dominican Republic but also to counter any attempted invasion from abroad.

The Cuban Army and Navy were mobilised to carry out General Pérez Dámera's 'plan'. The first action against the expeditionaries was to confiscate a shipment of weapons from a farm belonging to the minister of education, José Manuel Alemán, and to raid a flat that the expeditionaries had in the Sevilla hotel. The arsenal found on Minister Alemán's farm, which filled 13 army trucks, revealed an impressive array of war material acquired in the US and Argentina: some 3,000 Mauser rifles, 215 Thompson submachine guns, 50 German-patent machine guns, 10 automatic rifles, and Colt 45 pistols (for officers), along with several million rounds of ammunition. There were also 15 bazookas with 300 warheads, dozens of bombs (up to and including 300 lb types), 300 fragmentation bombs, 2 thousand pounds of dynamite, 300 rockets, 3 Brandt 81mm mortars,

2,000 hand grenades and 3 37mm cannons. All this war material was seized by the Cuban Army.

In tandem with Pérez Damera's actions, the American ambassador to Cuba, Henry Norweb, urged the aviators Rupert E. Waddel, Thomas Sawyer and Hollis Smith, the three Americans involved in the Cayo Confites affair, to return to the United States and abandon the expedition. The pilots responded to the call and returned home.

On the eve of the invasion, between 11 and 12 September, a tropical storm hit the Cayo Confites area, leaving the island completely flooded. This caused irreparable damage to weapons and ammunition, which were stored outdoors on the beach, ready to be loaded onto ships. As a result, the invasion was postponed until the end of that month. A few days later, on the 14th, a shootout occurred between rival political gangs in Havana, and it was then that President Grau decided to rid himself of the invasion and thus get the Americans off his back. Grau ordered General Pérez Dámera to take charge of the situation, aborting the invasion plans, arresting the expedition leaders and confiscating all the weapons. The Cuban Navy, which initially supported the invasion, had to follow presidential orders.

On 21 September, the leaders of the legion learned that the Cuban government no longer supported them, so they decided to leave the key and start the invasion. Thus, on 23 September, the expedition, led by General Juan Rodríguez, set sail from Cayo Confites and headed to Cayo Santa María, to the northwest, and from there to Cayo Guincho, the latter a British possession belonging to the Bahamas but located just off the Cuban coast. Soon, the three Cuban Navy frigates, led by the frigate *José Martí*, commanded by Frigate Captain Antonio Cuadra Garrote, were deployed to the area. Because the expedition was in a foreign possession, permission to disembark had to be requested. Meanwhile, the Cuban Navy frigates continued to patrol the area and when a landing was authorised, they found only 200 members of the expedition since the rest had escaped during the night in several boats.

The 200 who were detained on the island of Cayo Guincho stated that they wanted to abandon the 'adventure' and were thereupon disarmed and taken aboard the frigate *Antonio Maceo* back to Havana. Meanwhile, the frigates *José Martí* and *Máximo Gómez* set off in pursuit of the rest of the expedition members, conducting reconnaissance along the Haitian coast until ordered back to Cuba, where they finally spotted expedition vessels and the rest of the expeditionaries near the port of Antilla. Once intercepted, Captain Garrote of the *José Martí* ordered by loudspeaker to immediately stop their engines or he would open fire on them. The order was immediately obeyed by the fugitive boats. All the expedition members had already presented themselves on deck to surrender, except for one – Rolando Masferrer – who was finally persuaded to do so by General Rodríguez as commander of the expedition. Masferrer, however, addressing Captain Garrote, wanted to know what the status of the expedition members was, whether they were prisoners or simply being detained. The captain replied that he was uncertain regarding their status and added that he had orders to take them to Antilla, and from there they would be transferred to Havana. He thereupon asked Masferrer to surrender his weapon, and the prisoner reluctantly complied, handing over his .45 calibre pistol and two magazines.

530 men boarded the *Martí*, and another 600 did the same on the *Máximo Gómez*. Once in Antilla, the men were transferred to smaller boats while their seized weapons were unloaded, especially hundreds of hand grenades. From Antilla, they headed to Havana and then directly to Camp Columbia.

All weapons, ships and aircraft belonging to the expedition were subsequently seized. At around 9:30 p.m. on the evening of 31 July 1947, Lt Col Gonzalez-Chavez, the head of the CAEC, arrived at a training facility at Rancho Boyeros airport, by which time the entire invasion plan had come apart. Together with between 25 and 30 armed airmen, Gonzalez-Chavez immediately seized the PB4Y-1, two Lockheed RB-34s, two Douglas C-47s and two Cessna T-50s located at the airfield. The next day, CAEC crews started ferrying them to Camp Columbia, and by 11 August, these, along with all of the P-38s, had been summarily incorporated into the CAEC, complete with Cuban national insignia and serial numbers. By 30 September, the threat of invasion of the Dominican Republic had ended, with 90% of the combatants having been imprisoned, as well as several Cuban government officials who had supported that legion.

While a prisoner at Camp Columbia, Juan Bosch declared a hunger strike until all the expedition members were released. After an agreement between General Pérez Damera and Bosch, the prisoners were set free, and the leaders of the movement began negotiations with the Cuban government for the return of the confiscated weapons. Given the refusal of the Cuban government to return the seized materiel to the expedition members, the president of Guatemala, Juan José Arévalo, intervened, claiming ownership of them. In the end, nothing was returned, and all the booty remained in the Cuban Armed Forces.

In the final analysis, the only thing that the Caribbean Legion achieved was to accelerate the military expansion plans of the Dominican Armed Forces, which had begun in January of that year. One of the first measures undertaken by Trujillo was the expansion of several airfields and airports in order to enable them to accommodate large aircraft while also improving their communications systems. The Dominican Navy, meanwhile, acquired five corvettes from Canada. The purchase of aerial reconnaissance equipment, including Fairchild K-20 cameras, which had been authorised to be installed on military aircraft to spy on Cuba, was installed on Lockheed P-38s and a PBY-5A Catalina. These Dominican military aircraft carried out several photographic reconnaissance flights over Havana and Cayo Confites.

At that time, Dominican Military Aviation had Lockheed P-38L/M Lightning fighters; C-45, AT-11, C-47, C-46 and PBY-5A Catalina transport aircraft; and PT-17, BT-13A and AT-6C/D trainers. The P-38s and AT-6C/Ds conducted daily air patrols during the legion's threatened invasion, with two daytime and two nighttime flights per day starting on 16 June 1947. Other aircraft were also used in these patrols, including BT-13s and especially the PBY-5A Catalinas, which had a greater flight range. Dominican intelligence had managed to obtain precise information about the places where the legion troops would land, and as a result, several P-38s were deployed to the La Vega airfield, in the northern part of the country, where a FAERA C-46 was supposed to land with 30 guerrillas.

The three Cuban Navy frigates that participated in the capture of the Cayo Confites expeditionaries: F301 *José Martí*, former U.S. Navy PF-40 *USS Eugene* (top), F302 *Antonio Maceo*, former U.S. Navy PF-67 *USS Peoria* (centre) and F303 *Máximo Gómez*, former U.S. Navy PF-14 *USS Grant Island* (bottom). (Rogali collection)

6

THE CUBAN NAVAL AIR FORCE (FAN)

The birth of Cuban naval aviation

Although the aviation wing of the Cuban Navy has always been a small force, it deserves a separate chapter. Because Cuba is an island, it has always needed not only a navy but also aerial means to patrol its coasts. According to the Cuban naval historian Maximino Gómez Álvarez, efforts to develop Cuban naval aviation began on 17 September 1925, although it was not until ten years later that it was organised as a body within the general organisation of the Navy, establishing its offices and workshops at the Rancho Boyeros airport.

Cuba's first naval aircraft was an Atlantic Aircraft (Fokker) F.9 Universal with floats, provided by the CAEC in January 1928. President Machado asked the Cuban Congress to authorise funds to buy six more hydroplanes, either F.9s or Loenings, for the naval air wing, but it was not possible for political and monetary reasons.

The development of a naval air force was slow since additional aircraft were not acquired until 1935, when a De Havilland DH.60GM Moth, a Curtiss Fledgling and a Keystone-Loening K-84 Commuter were obtained, despite having a small budget. The Moth had been donated by a pilot – Second Lieutenant René Baserrate Miró. The following year, a Waco 10/GXE and a Lockheed Sirius 8A were purchased, the latter christened *4 de Septiembre*, in reference to the political movement led by the then Sergeant Fulgencio Batista which seized power on 4 September 1933.

The first training course for naval aviators was carried out at the Military Aviation School at Camp Columbia with five graduate officers from the Mariel Naval Academy: Ensigns Plazaola, Garcerán, Belisario Rodríguez, San Pedro and Pérez Terrada. In 1935, the Naval Aviation School was established.

The pioneers of Cuban naval aviation were Captain Pedro Duarte, Commander Eduardo López Calderón, Frigate Captain Ernesto Usatorres, who later became the head of Cuban naval aviation, Commander Gustavo Novo and Captain Enrique Fernández Vallín. Cuban naval aviation, despite being a small force, would perform several epic long-haul flights that undoubtedly enhanced its prestige, as can be seen below.

The first aircraft of Cuban naval aviation, an Atlantic Aircraft (Fokker) F.9 Universal. It bore the words *M.G. de Cuba* (*Marina de Guerra de Cuba*, Cuban Navy) painted on both sides of the fuselage. (P.R.B.J. Collection)

A De Havilland D.H.60GM Gipsy Moth, serial number N-I-1, with (from left to right in both photos) student René Bassarate Miró, instructor Lt. Ernesto Usatorres y Ubieta, and student Ensign Gustavo Novo y Saborido in 1934 at Rancho Boyeros airport. (P.R.B.J. Collection)

Some sailors assigned to Cuban naval aviation posing with several mechanics alongside a Curtiss Fledgling, serial number N-I-2. (P.R.B.J. Collection)

A Keystone-Loening K.84 Commuter flying boat. Cuban naval aviation received a similar aircraft with serial number 3. (goldenwingsmuseum.com)

The Lockheed Sirius 8A, serial number 10, nicknamed *4 de Septiembre*, that made the flight connecting Cuba to Seville in Spain in 1936 (left). The pilot who made the crossing, Lieutenant Antonio Menéndez Peláez, departing the Sirius cockpit (right). (P.R.B.J. Collection)

Pioneers of Cuban naval aviation. From left to right, Captain Pedro Duarte, Commander Eduardo López Calderón, Frigate Captain Ernesto Usatorres, who became head of the Cuban Naval Air Force (FAN), Commander Gustavo Novo and Captain Enrique Fernández Vallín. (Asociación para la Investigación y Difusión de la Historia Naval de Cuba)

A postcard widely distributed in Cuba commemorating Lt Menendez's epic flight. (Internet)

Lieutenant Menéndez's epic flight from Cuba to Spain

A Lockheed Sirius 8A belonging to the then *Cuban Aviación de la Marina de Guerra* (Naval Aviation) was used by Lieutenant Antonio Menéndez Peláez to make a long-haul flight between Rancho Boyeros airport in Cuba and Seville, Spain, between 9 January and 14 February 1936. The Sirius made the following stops on its long flight: Camagüey in Cuba, Caracas in Venezuela, Trinidad, Guyana, French Guiana, and Belém, São Luiz, Fortaleza and Natal in Brazil. Once in Natal, Lt Menéndez stayed for a week in order to solve some technical problems in the Sirius and to wait for better weather conditions. The aircraft then crossed the Atlantic Ocean, landing in Bathurst, Gambia, in Africa. From there, it flew to Cabo Juby in Spanish West Africa and from there directly to Seville, Spain. The return trip was made in an ocean liner from Santander to Havana.

The Pan-American Flight for Columbus Lighthouse

In 1937, Cuban naval aviation received a Stinson SR-9D Reliant, which was christened with the name *La Niña* (the name of one of the three caravels used by Christopher Columbus in 1492 during his first trip to America). This aircraft, together with two other Reliants, one from the CAEC and the other a civilian aircraft, plus a Dominican military aviation Curtiss CW-19R, participated in an air race called the Pan American Flight for Columbus Lighthouse. The participants of the race were as follows:

- Cuban naval aviation Stinson SR-9D Reliant, serial number 51, named *La Niña*, flown by Lt Feliciano Risech Amat with the mechanic Sergeant Roberto Medina.
- CAEC Stinson SR-9D Reliant, serial number 104, named *Santa María*, crewed by Lt Antonio Menéndez Peláez with the mechanic Corporal Manuel Naranjo.
- Cuban civilian Stinson SR-9D Reliant, named *La Pinta*, flown by pilot Lt Alfredo Jiménez Alum and Sergeant Pedro Castillo as mechanic.
- Dominican Army Aviation Corps Curtiss CW-19R, named *Colón*, with Major Frank Féliz Miranda as pilot and Sergeant Julio Ernesto Tejada Matos as mechanic.

The flight started at 9:50 a.m. on 12 November 1937, when all four aircraft took off from the Miraflores airfield in the Dominican Republic bound for San Juan, Puerto Rico. On the 14th of that month, they reached La Guaira airport in Maiquetía, near Caracas, Venezuela.

Then on the 17th they all flew to Port of Spain in Trinidad. From there, the flight headed to Paramaribo in Dutch Guiana. On the 19th they reached the city of Belém in Brazil, and on the 21st they arrived in Fortaleza, also in Brazil. Then they visited several other Brazilian cities: Natal, Recife, Bahía and Rio de Janeiro. On the 29th, the flight reached Porto Alegre, Brazil. Then the trip continued with stops in Montevideo, Uruguay, and Buenos Aires, Argentina.

On 8 December, they left for Santiago de Chile and from there to La Paz, Bolivia, where they arrived on the 13th. On the 15th, flying through dense fog towards Peru, the Stinson *La Niña* of Cuban naval aviation was lost. The Curtiss *Colón* and the Stinson *La Pinta* landed in Pisco, while the Stinson *Santa María* landed in Lima. An intense search for the Stinson *La Niña* began, but it was not found, so the remaining aircraft met in Lima. It was learned that the missing aircraft had had problems with its radio and had landed safely in the San Juan Valley. Once solved, the Stinson *La Niña* arrived in Lima, and from there the four aircraft reached Bogotá, Colombia, on 26 December.

On the 29th, the four planes took off towards Panama, but shortly after taking off, the three Cuban Stinsons crashed into the mountains in the El Valle area, near Cali, killing all their crew members. The Dominican Curtiss crew continued on their journey to Panama, completely unaware of what had happened, only learning about the tragedy when they landed in Panama City.

The crews of the four aircraft that participated in the Pan-American Flight for Columbus Lighthouse. (Open source)

The four aircraft that participated in the epic Pan-American Flight for Columbus Lighthouse. From left to right: The Dominican Curtiss CW-19R *Colón* and the three Stinson SR-9D Reliants, CAEC serial number 104 *Santa María*, the civilian *La Pinta*, and the naval aviation serial number 51 *La Niña*. Only the Curtiss would complete the flight, as the three Reliants were lost in a tragic accident with the death of all their crews. (Open source)

The Cuban naval aviation Stinson SR-9D Reliant, serial number 51, *La Niña*, in Lima, Peru, during the Columbus Lighthouse Goodwill Flight (left). The aircraft eventually crashed in Cali, Colombia. A closer view of the *La Niña* emblem on the Cuban naval aviation Stinson (right). (P.R.B.J. Collection)

Photo taken in Cali, Colombia, at the spot where the Cuban pilots of the Pan American Flight for Columbus Lighthouse lost their lives. The two naval officers are Commander Montenegro (centre) and Captain Rivery (second from the left). (Asociación para la Investigación y Difusión de la Historia Naval de Cuba)

The first new aircraft

In March 1938, Cuban naval aviation, now officially designated the Cuban Naval Air Force (*Fuerza Aérea Naval*, FAN), received three brand-new WACO UMF-3 biplanes capable of being armed with machine guns and a small payload of bombs.

Aircraft acquisitions in the 1940s, Lend-Lease Program and World War II

During the Second World War, the so-called Punta Gorda Naval Air Base was established at the Port of Mariel, whence it was subsequently known as the Parlá Aeronaval Base, or simply the Parlá Base, in homage to the pioneer of Cuban aviation.

The Parlá Base had two runways, one of 2,000 x 150 metres and the other of 1,000 x 100 metres. There was also an aviation fuel depot with three 20,000-gallon fuel tanks, all of them underground. It had a detachable hangar brought from Camp Columbia that was substantially rebuilt and expanded, providing a 1,050 m2 concrete apron in front. A concrete ramp 80 metres long x 20 metres wide was also built, of which 45 metres extended into the sea. It also had buildings with a guardhouse, headquarters offices and a control tower with all the technological advances of the time. The base also had areas for workshops, garages, a dining room for officers and enlisted men, meeting rooms, a cafeteria for officers and enlisted men, a medical dispensary and infirmary, as well as storage warehouses for all types of equipment, spare parts and ammunition. Two pavilions for enlisted personnel with 160 beds and one for officers were also built, as well as 12 additional rooms for pilots in service. Within the base, all the units were connected with auxiliary streets 5 metres wide, built of Telford-Macadam, including the installation of a new drainage and sewage system and an aqueduct for a daily supply of 40,000 gallons of water.

During the 1940s, the Naval Air Force received a significant number of aircraft, as follows:

- A Howard DGA-8 and a Howard DGA-15W for utility transport, in 1940.
- Three Ford 4-AT Trimotor aircraft for transport, between 1941 and 1946.

The Cuban Naval Air Force played a very important role during World War II in patrolling the country's coastline, performing escort missions for merchant ships, pursuing German submarines and locating and supporting the rescue of shipwrecked crews. In order to carry out these important missions, the Cuban Naval Air Force received the following aircraft through the US Lend-Lease Program:

The Cuban Naval Air Force's three Waco UMF-3s, serial numbers 26, 27, and 28, acquired in March 1938. (National Waco Club)

Lieutenant Juan Rios Montenegro and Sergeant Frank Medina standing in front of a Cuban Naval Air Force Howard DGA-15W, serial number 54. (AirHistory.net)

Table 3: Lend-Lease Aircraft for the FAN[1]

Model	Quantity	Previous identification	Cuban Naval Air Force Number
Grumman JRF-5 Goose	2	BuAer 39747 BuAer 39748	56 57
Vought-Sikorsky OS2U-3 Kingfisher	3	BuAer 5932 BuAer 5933 BuAer 5934	30, later 50 31, later 51 32, later 52
Naval Air Factory N3N-1	3	BuAer 0688 BuAer 0953 BuAer 0962	1 2 3
Curtiss SO3C Seamew	3	JW698 (*) JW699 (*) JW691 (*)	45 46 47

(*) British serial numbers. These aircraft did not receive USN serial numbers.

With the outbreak of World War II and the entry of the United States and then Cuba into the conflict, naval aviator officers were sent on scholarships to the US Navy Base in Pensacola, Florida, on 7 July 1942, where they received intensive flight training. These officers were Pedro Duarte García, Eddy López Calderón, Ernesto Usatorres Ubieta, the then head of the Cuban Naval Air Force, Gustavo Novo Saborido, and Enrique Fernández Vallín.

Below: From left to right, Cuban Naval Air Force officers Pedro Duarte García, Eddy López Calderón, Ernesto Usatorres Ubieta, then head of the Naval Air Force, Gustavo Novo Saborido and Enrique Fernández Vallín at the US Navy Naval Aviation Station in Pensacola, Florida, on 7 July 1942, where they received intensive training with the outbreak of the Second World War. (Asociación para la Investigación y Difusión de la Historia Naval de Cuba)

Officers and NCOs of the U.S. Navy's VP-62 Squadron posing with Vought Kingfisher aircraft on Cayo Francés, Cuba, during World War II. (Asociación para la Investigación y Difusión de la Historia Naval de Cuba)

The Cuban Naval Air Force received three Vought-Sikorsky OS2U-3 Kingfishers, which received the initial serial numbers 30, 31 and 32 (top) and later the numbers 50, 51 and 52 (bottom). (Historia de la Aviación Militar Cubana/HAMC & P.R.B.J. Collection)

It was also during the Second World War that a seaplane station was built in Cayo Francés on Cuba's north coast and another for airships on the Isla de Pinos off the country's south coast, whose main objective was anti-submarine combat. US Navy Squadron VP-62 was stationed there with Vought Kingfisher aircraft. The participation of the Cuban Naval Air Force in anti-submarine missions in the waters of the Caribbean and the Gulf of Mexico was very important, given the few resources it had at that time. In total, the Cuban Naval Air Force escorted 114 ships travelling 83,000 miles in convoy and patrol services until 7 May 1945. Their aircraft flew a total of 853:20 hours. They also carried out several search and rescue (SAR) missions. On no occasion did they sight and attack German submarines, however. All of their aircraft operated from the then naval air bases of Rancho Boyeros near Havana and Mariel. Many naval pilots received flight training at the Pensacola Naval Air School in Florida, United States.

In 1949, the Cuban government approached the US State Department with an aircraft request for the Naval Air Force. The Cubans wanted to invest around US$9.9 million in the project in order to modernise their relatively small naval aviation force. The request included aircraft like Curtiss SC-1 Seahawks, Vought-Sikorsky OS2U-3 Kingfishers, Boeing-Stearman N2S-5 Kaydets, North American SNJ-5 Texans, Martin PBM-5A Mariners and Consolidated PBY-6A

The FAN also received two Grumman JRF-5 Goose aircraft (top) through the US Lend-Lease Program in the 1940s, in addition to three NAF N3N-1s (bottom) and three Curtiss SO3C Seamews to patrol the Cuban coasts. (P.R.B.J. Collection)

Catalinas. Apparently, most of the aircraft types mentioned were not available at that time; instead, the Cuban Naval Air Force received Avenger torpedo bombers and some Catalinas.

The American Solidarity Flight

Another epic feat of Cuban naval aviation was the so-called American Solidarity Flight, which took place between 12 October 1940 and 15 February 1941. This flight covered almost 30,400 kilometres throughout America and involved some 200 flight hours and 88 landings through 20 different countries.

The aircraft chosen for the flight was the Howard DGA-15, serial number 54, of the Naval Air Force, nicknamed *Teniente Menéndez*, and its crew was composed of Naval Reserve Frigate Ensign Oscar Augusto Rivery Ortíz as flight chief and navigator, Naval Reserve Sub Lieutenant Juan de Dios Ríos Montenegro as pilot, and aviation mechanic Third Sergeant Francisco Medina Pérez.

The flight began in Havana with a stop in Camagüey, Cuba. Then followed Port-au-Prince (Haiti), Ciudad Trujillo (Dominican Rep.), San Juan (Puerto Rico), La Guaira and Garipito (Venezuela), Port of Spain (Trinidad and Tobago), Paramaribo (Guyana), Belém, Parnahiba, Ceará, Pernambuco, Salvador, Victoria, Rio de Janeiro, São Paulo and Campo Grande (Brazil), Asunción (Paraguay), Alegretto, Rivera and Montevideo (Uruguay), Buenos Aires, San Luis and Mendoza (Argentina), Santiago, Vallenar, Copiapó, Antofagasta and Arica (Chile), La Paz (Bolivia), Arica again, Moliendo, Lima, Chiclayo and Talara (Peru), Guayaquil (Ecuador), Papayán, Cali and Medellín (Colombia), Panama City (Panama), San José (Costa Rica), Managua (Nicaragua), Tegucigalpa (Honduras), San Salvador (El Salvador), Guatemala City (Guatemala), Tapachula, Veracruz, México City and Tampico (México), Brownsville, Galveston, New Orleans, Mobile, Atlanta, Greenborough, Washington DC, New York, Charleston and Miami (USA) and finally Havana in Cuba.

Final acquisitions in the 1950s

Based on some photographic evidence, at least two PBY-5As were acquired in the early 1950s. In 1952, another two PBY-5A Catalinas and in 1954, two Convair OA-10 Catalina amphibians were incorporated. In 1956, through the MAP programme, the Naval Air Force received seven Grumman TBM-3S2 Avenger torpedo bombers.

On 23 June 1957, at the Pensacola Naval Air Base in Florida, Captain Mario Rubio Baró, head of the Cuban Naval Air Force, received a new Catalina aircraft. On that occasion, the following FAN officers were there, too: Commanders Juarrero and Eddy López Calderón, Captain Juarrero (Junior) and Commander Octavio González Muñoz.

The three crew members of the Cuban Naval Air Force's Howard DGA-15W, serial number 54, that carried out the American Solidarity Goodwill Flight visiting 22 countries in 1940: from left to right, Lieutenant Juan Rios Montenegro, Commander Oscar Rivery and Sergeant Frank Medina (top left) (P.R.B.J. Collection). The same aircraft preparing to take off after a stopover in New York (bottom left). Frigate Ensign Oscar Augusto Rivery Ortíz (right). (Nuestra Fuerza Aérea Histórica)

Cuban Naval Air Force officers pose in front of an OA-10 Catalina delivered to the force in 1957 in Pensacola, Florida. (Asociación para la Investigación y Difusión de la Historia Naval de Cuba)

A Cuban Naval Air Force Consolidated OA-10A Catalina (left) and a PBY-5A, serial number 190 (right). (P.R.B.J. Collection)

A Naval Air Force Grumman TBM-3C2 Avenger, serial number 62, at Rancho Boyeros airport in Havana (left) and an Avenger, serial number 60, in flight (right). (Historia de la Aviación Militar Cubana/HAMC)

A Naval Air Force PBY-5A Catalina flying over the frigate F301 *José Martí* of the Cuban Navy in the Bay of Havana in the late 1950s (top). One of the PBY-5As of the Naval Air Force (bottom). (Asociación para la Investigación y Difusión de la Historia Naval de Cuba)

The final acquisition was to be a pair of Sikorsky S.55 helicopters for SAR duties, but they were not delivered due to the deteriorating political situation in Cuba in the late 1950s. The revolutionary government took power in 1959, and shortly thereafter the Naval Air Force was dissolved as an independent corps, becoming an integral part of the Revolutionary Air Force (FAR) attached to the Revolutionary Navy (MGR).

Navy Captain Ernesto Julio Usatorres Ubieta

A key personality in the history of Cuban naval aviation was Captain Ernesto Julio Usatorres Ubieta. He was born in Havana, Cuba, on 7 November 1908. He graduated from high school at the Havana Institute in 1926. He then studied law at the University of Havana for two years (1926-1928). The closure of the university by the government interrupted his studies.

He then passed the entrance examinations of the Army Military Aviation School in 1929 and became a cadet. He graduated in 1930, and he served about four years in the CAEC as a second lieutenant pilot. In 1934, the chief of the General Staff of the Navy, Captain Ángel Aurelio González, offered him the opportunity to reorganise and develop Cuban naval aviation. He accepted the challenge and was transferred to the Navy. Eventually he became the head of the Cuban naval aviation for three periods, the last one from 10 March 1952 until the summer of 1956, when he was a captain.

In August 1956, Captain Usatorres was assigned to take the Naval Command Course for foreign naval officers at the US Naval War College in the city of Newport, Rhode Island. He graduated on 2 June 1957. However, he retired in 1958. In 1961, he went to the United States, where he died on 17 November 1996.

Top: A Naval Air Force Vought-Sikorsky OS2U-3 Kingfisher in 1948, at Camagüey airport (top) (James C. Sanders via H.A.M.C.). The three Naval Air Force Grumman Avengers at Camp Columbia in the late 1950s. (H.A.M.C.)

Centre: Cuban naval pilots at the US Naval Aviation Air Station in Pensacola, Florida, where they received flight training (left). Captain Ernesto Julio Usatorres Ubieta (right). (Open source)

Bottom: The official emblem of the FAN (left). Cuban Naval Air Force pilot wings (right). (Open source)

7

THE CAEC IN THE LATE 1940S AND EARLY 1950S

The Cuban Army Air Corps was able to incorporate a wide array of combat and transport aircraft that the government had seized from the expedition members of the failed invasion of the Dominican Republic in 1947. They are detailed in the table below.

Table 4: FAERA aircraft incorporated into the CAEC[1]

Aircraft	Nr. of Aircraft	Previous Identification	CAEC number
Lockheed P-38M Lightning	3	44-53100, NC67849 44-27258, NX67863 44-53082, NX62805	121 123 124
Lokheed P-38L-5-VN Lightning	2	43-50312, NL5016N 43-50310, NL75666	122 126
Lockheed P-38L-5-LO Lightning	1	44-27145	125
Consolidated PB4Y-1 (B-24L-15-CO) Liberator	1	44-41740, BuA 65325	400
North American B-25C-15-NA Mitchell	1	42-32385	301
North American B-25H-5-NA Mitchell	1	43-4536	300
Lockheed RB-34 (PV-1) Ventura	2	41-38020 41-38032, BuA 48529	214 215
Curtiss C-46A-45-CU Commando	1	42-96591	Cuban civilian registration CU-P153
Douglas C-47-DL Skytrain	2	41-18535, NC-56001 41-38579, NC-66113	203 204

The P-38 fighter operations in the CAEC

As a result of the seizure of all the aircraft from the failed Cayo Confites operation, the CAEC strengthened its fleet, as noted in the previous chapter. The P-38 Lightning fighters, which were state-of-the-art aircraft at that time, were in service for a few years, but as they did not have maintenance manuals or spare parts, they were withdrawn from service in the early 1950s. P-38M, serial number 124, was badly damaged in a hurricane in 1948, while P-38M, serial number 121, was destroyed in a fatal accident on 29 January 1951, killing Lt Joaquín Varona Acosta. In addition, on 19 May 1950, P-38L, serial number 125, crewed by Lt Rafael Lima Silva, made an emergency landing due to engine problems at a country club near Havana. The pilot was injured and the aircraft was destroyed. According to an American intelligence report in June 1950, there were only two P-38s left in service, with a third one currently inoperable. It is believed that in 1953, when the first F-47 Thunderbolt arrived, none of the P-38s were still in operation. Some of the pilots who flew them were Lieutenants Hubert Masmontet, Miguel Matamoros del Valle, Guillermo Corvo Alzamora, Enrique Carreras Rolas and Rafael Lima Silva. The P-38Ls were single-seat day fighters, while the P-38Ms, which were painted completely black, were two-seat night fighters without radar.

In 1947, the following pilot officers graduated from the Military Aviation School: Juan Brito García, Roberto Carrillo Castillo, Rolando Cossio Soto, Luis Cosme Toribio, Héctor Hernández, Osvaldo Hernández Suárez, Manuel Iglesias Ramírez, Raúl Planás, Joaquín Varona, Manuel Villafaña Martínez, Antonio Michel Yabor Justiz and Mario Zúñiga Rivas.

Reports presented to Congress around this time regarding the use of the P-38 fighters merely indicate the total air mileage of each type of fighter per fiscal year without providing the cumulative numbers. These annual reports demonstrate that the Naval Air Force made active use of the P-38s between 1947 and 1950, when the reports abruptly stopped, with the following mileages reported: 1947 = 5,126 miles, 1948 = 4,083 miles, 1949 = 3,663 miles and 1950 = 11,813 miles. Although the P-38s were fighters, they were never armed, not even during their CAEC service, and consequently, they never saw action of any kind.

During the period 1947-1948, when General Eulogio Cantillo Porrás was head of the CAEC, the runways were paved at Camp Columbia. In 1948, the old Almendares Hotel was acquired and remodelled to house the CAEC headquarters, its offices and its squadrons, with large dining rooms, rooms for officers and dormitories for enlisted men, classrooms for cadets, a club and an open-air cinema.

In 1948, the following pilot officers graduated from the Military Aviation School: Raúl Cross Quintana, René García Fernández, Jorge González Barrera, Aurelio Martínez Leiro, Emilio Pérez, Claudio Rey Moriñas, René Travieso Plá and Raúl Vianello Alacán.

The American Republics Program (ARP) for the CAEC and other acquisitions

The U.S. government's ARP Program was launched with the intention of standardising the tactical and support aircraft of the Western hemispheric air forces. Cuba was one of a number of countries that benefited from this project.

At the beginning of the ARP implementation, Cuba was to have received eight Republic P-47D Thunderbolt fighters, but this was not approved by the programme administrators. In fact, at that time the CAEC owned the P-38 Lightning fighters that had been seized from the Caribbean Legion. In any case, other types of aircraft were approved for delivery to the CAEC between 1946 and 1956:

- Four North American B-25J Mitchell medium bombers.
- Two Convair OA-10 Catalinas, which were transferred to the Naval Air Force.
- 12 Douglas C-47s, including one VIP-outfitted Hi-Per DC-3 for presidential use.
- Six Beechcraft twins, including two AT-7s, two AT-11s, one F-2B and one UC-45F.

The last acquisition of the CAEC before officially becoming the FAEC was that of six Beechcraft 35 Bonanzas to expand airmail services on the island.

Five of the six Lockheed P-38s seized from FAERA and incorporated into the CAEC: a P-38M, serial number 123 (top left); a P-38L, serial number 122 (top right); a P-38M, serial number 124 (bottom left); and a P-38M, serial number 121, and a P-38L, serial number 125, in the background (bottom right). (P.R.B.J. Collection and Memorias del Ministerio de Guerra y Marina)

On the right, the Consolidated P4Y-1 Liberator serial number 400 of the CAEC already in a derelict state in 1948. In the background the effects of Hurricane Easy of that year can be seen as a C-46 sits atop several aircraft, including a B-25C Mitchell, a C-47 and a P-38 Lightning. (Nuestra Fuerza Aérea Histórica)

This Douglas C-47-DL Skytrain, serial number 203, nicknamed *El Viejo Pancho* (The Old Pancho), was one of two C-47s seized from FAERA and incorporated into the CAEC in 1947. (P.R.B.J. Collection)

In 1947-1948, when General Eulogio Cantillo Porrás (right) was head of the CAEC, the runways at Camp Columbia were paved. In 1948, the old Almendares Hotel (left) was acquired and remodelled to house the CAEC headquarters. (Open source)

The ramp of the main air base at Camp Columbia, near Havana, in the late 1940s. A variety of CAEC aircraft can be seen: a Boeing-Stearman PT-17 Kaydet and a Beech UC-45F in the front row; behind them are BT-13 and AT-6 trainers; and in the background, a Douglas C-47, a PBY-5A Catalina, P-38 fighters and B-25 Mitchell bombers. (Rod Simpson)

Three North American B-25J Mitchell medium bombers of the FAEC at Camp Columbia in 1956. (Historia de la Aviación Militar Cubana/HAMC)

Four Douglas C-47s of the FAEC, with the insignia adopted in 1955: Serial numbers 201 (top left), 206 (top right), 210 (bottom left) and 204 (bottom right), the latter at Batista Field. (P.R.B.J. Collection)

A FAEC Beech AT-11, serial number 160 (above), and a group of pilots posing with Beech UC-45F, serial number 213 (below). (Albert Grandolini collection via Tom Cooper)

CAEC pilots posing with an AT-6C Texan (left). A military pilot about to board an AT-6C for a routine training mission (right). (José Ramón de la Torre)

The B-25 Mitchell operations

The CAEC's first two B-25 Mitchell bombers were those seized from FAERA, one a B-25C and the other a B-25H. The B-25H was a variant with a solid nose equipped with a 75mm cannon, and incredibly, when the Legion del Caribe acquired this plane from the company specialising in sales of war surplus material for the civilian market, Universal Aviation Co. of Tulsa, Oklahoma, it was still equipped with the cannon! Reportedly, the 75mm cannon remained installed even when it was put up for sale on the civilian market, as the selling company did not know how to remove it from the plane. Nevertheless, the cannon was not used when in service with the CAEC.

As for the B-25C model, according to sources consulted, it was part of a batch of five B-25Cs that had been converted to B-25Gs and had also received a solid nose armed with a 75mm cannon. However, we were unable to determine whether this plane also came equipped with the cannon.

A FAEC North American B-25J Mitchell, serial number 303, at Camp Columbia. (Nuestra Fuerza Aérea Histórica)

A B-25J, serial number 305, also at Camp Columbia. It is missing the upper machine gun turret (top left). (P.R.B.J. Collection)

In 1952, a B-25J, serial number 302, made a belly landing at Camp Columbia. The aircraft was later repaired. (History of Cuban Military Aviation/HAMC)

In 1947, within the ARP program, Cuba requested the United States supply four B-25Js equipped with full armament, which would bring the total inventory to six B-25s to be used for equipping the Escuadrón de Bombardeo.

In the early years, the only B-25C in the inventory, with serial number 301, was written off due to serious corrosion problems. In 1948, the same B-25C was damaged on the ground by a hurricane together with other aircraft. However, it seems that it was repaired and continued in active service for a few more years. In the first half of the 1950s, three B-25s – those in better condition – underwent maintenance work by technicians from a USAF mission, while a fourth, which required more elaborate maintenance, was sent for this purpose to the USAF Mobile Air Depot in Mobile, Alabama.

When the local air force was already known by its new designation, the FAEC, the unit that operated the B-25s was called the *Escuadrón de Bombardeo Ligero '4 de Septiembre'* ('4th September' Light Bomber Squadron) at Camp Columbia. Once there was a request from the FAEC to transform the B-25s into the TB-25 training version. Thus, one of the surviving B-25s was disarmed in 1954.

An FAEC B-25J Mitchell taxiing at Camp Columbia, with two parked F-47D Thunderbolts in the background. The upper machine gun turret has been removed and its bomb bay doors are open. (Historia de la Aviación Militar Cubana/HAMC)

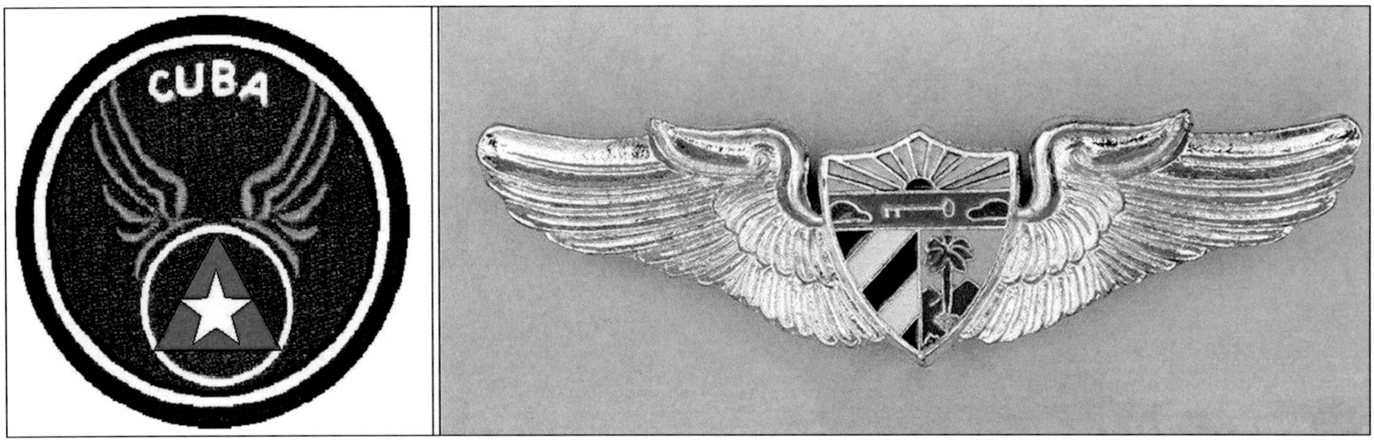

The official emblem of the CAEC (left) and Cuban military pilot wings (right). (Open source)

In January 1956, while acquiring the B-26 Invader, the four surviving B-25s (three B-25Js and one B-25H) were used as part of the payment for the B-26s. Even so, during the first years of the fight against Castro's guerrillas, the four B-25s, together with F-47 fighters, were used to carry out maritime patrol flights using Santiago de Cuba and Camagüey as bases.

Table 5: CAEC/FAEC B-25 Mitchell fleet[2]

Model	Previous Identification	CAEC/FAEC Serial Number
B-25H	43-4536	300
B-25C	42-32385	301
B-25J	44-30348	302
B-25J	44-30326	303
B-25J	44-30095	304
B-25J	44-25848	305

After returning to the U.S., the three B-25Js and one B-25H were exported to the Uruguayan Air Force, with the B-25H still carrying the 75mm cannon in its nose!

Efforts to acquire combat and transport aircraft in the early 1950s

Between 1951 and 1953, the Cuban government made requests for combat aircraft from its American counterpart, submitting a list of its requirements:

- 12 Lockheed F-80C Shooting Star tactical fighters
- Six Lockheed T-33A advanced trainers/light attack aircraft
- Five North American T-28A Trojan advanced trainers/light attack aircraft

One of three B-25Js that belonged to the CAEC and later served in the Uruguayan Air Force, with serial number 162 (above). The only B-25H in CAEC service, where it bore serial number 300, belonged originally to the FAERA in the failed Cayo Confites expedition and ended its days in the Uruguayan Air Force with serial number 164. It was active until its retirement in 1965 (below). (Albert Grandolini collection via Tom Cooper)

The request even said that if the F-80Cs were not available, they could be replaced by North American F-51D Mustangs, Vought F4U Corsairs, Grumman F8F Bearcats, F9F Panthers or McDonnell F2H Banshees. As if all that were not enough, the Cubans also requested:

- Nine North American B-25 Mitchell or Douglas B-26C Invader medium bombers
- Four Consolidated PBY-5A Catalinas
- 12 Fairchild C-82 Packet, Curtiss C-46D or Douglas C-47B transport aircraft

In response to this long list of orders, the American government replied that due to the Korean War, the F-80Cs, B-25Js, F-51Ds and C-82s were not available, offering instead only four PBY-5A Catalinas.

EPILOGUE

Cuban military aviation had, like the vast majority of the air forces in Latin America, a very humble beginning. It grew fitfully, as has been seen in this volume, but the interesting thing was that it was prepared to participate in aerial actions as early as the First World War, something that did not happen because the conflict ended before the Cuban squadron of aviators could be deployed in Europe. In the period between two world wars, Cuba's military aviation distinguished itself for a series of long-haul flights across the Americas, as did the small naval aviation force. Already in World War II, Cuba benefited from the Lend-Lease Program of the American government above all because it had to patrol its coasts against the threat of German submarines.

Following World War II, the CAEC benefited greatly from other American government programmes such as the ARP and the MDAP, acquiring modern fighters and medium bombers, which would later be used in the fight against the guerrillas in the mid-1950s.

APPENDIX

Table 6: CAEC aircraft types 1913-1952[1]

Aircraft	No. of aircraft	Serials	Role	Year of acquisition
Curtiss Model FS	1	-	Flying boat	1913
Morane-Saulnier G	1	-	Monoplane	1915
Curtiss JN-4D Jenny	6	1 to 6	Primary trainer	1918
Curtiss JN-6H Jenny	2	7 & 8	Primary trainer	1924
Vought QO-2 Corsair	9	7 to 15	Fighter	1924
De Havilland D.H.4M-1	6	11 to 16	Light bomber	1924
Consolidated PT-3 Husky	10	1 to 8, 11 & 12	Primary trainer	1928
Curtiss Wright P-6S Hawk	5	9, 10, 15, 16 & 18	Fighter	1929
Vought O2U-1A Corsair	6	16 to 21	Observation	1929
WACO PCF-2	1	?	Observation	1931
WACO 9	2	?	Trainer	1932
WACO 10	2	13 & 14	Light transport	1932
Vought O2U-3A Corsair	11	24 to 34	Observation	1933
Curtiss Wright 35A Hawk I	4	19 to 22	Fighter	1933
Aeronca C-3	1	?	Light trainer	1933
WACO UBF-2	1	?	Observation/trainer	1933
WACO S3HD-A	1	23	Attack/Light bomber	1934
WACO PBF-2	1	?	Observation	1934
Curtiss Robin	1	?	Transport	1935
Bellanca Model 66-75 Airbus	1	103	Attack	1935
WACO CPF-6	1	?	Observation	1936
WACO ZPF-6	1	?	Observation	1936
Stinson SR-9D Reliant	1	104	Transport	1937
Curtiss-Wright CW-19R All Metal	5	50 to 54, two of them reserialled as 101 and 102	Fighter/light bomber	1937
Stearman Model A73B1	7	43 to 49	Primary trainer	1939
Aeronca 65TC Chief (*)	4	34 to 37	Observation/Liaison	1941
Curtiss-Wright SNC-1 (+)	5	55 to 59	Fighter	1942
Boeing-Stearman PT-17	6	38 to 43	Primary trainer	1942

Aircraft	No. of aircraft	Serials	Role	Year of acquisition
Vultee BT-13A Valiant	9	66 to 74	Basic trainer	1942-1943
North American AT-6C Texan	9	102 to 110	Advanced trainer/Light attack	1942-1943
Aeronca L-3B	6	1 to 6	Observation/Liaison	1943
Boeing-Stearman N2S-4 Kaydet	3	44 to 46	Primary trainer	1943
North American AT-6F Texan	10	111 to 120	Advanced trainer/Light attack	1945
Beechcraft S.17D Staggerwing	1	1	VIP transport	1945
Stinson 105	1	2	VIP transport	1945
Stinson 108 Voyager	1	3	VIP transport	1945
Boeing-Stearman N2S-4 Kaydet	3	47 to 49	Primary trainer	1946
Douglas C-47A/B/D	11	200, 201, 202, 203, 205, 206, 207, 208, 210, 211 & 212	Transport	1946-1956
Douglas Hi-Per DC-3/C-53	1	209	Presidential Transport	1954
Lockheed P-38L Lightning (#)	3	122, 125 & 126	Fighter	1947
Lockheed P-38M Lightning (#)	3	121, 123 & 124	Night Fighter	1947
North American B-25H (#)	1	300	Medium bomber	1947
North American B-25C (#)	1	301	Medium bomber	1947
North American B-25J Mitchell	4	302 to 305	Medium bomber	1947
Lockheed RB-34 Ventura (#)	2	214 & 215	Patrol bomber	1947
Consolidated PB4Y-1 Liberator (#)	1	400	Heavy bomber	1947
Douglas C-47 (#)	2	203 & 204	Transport	1947
Curtiss C-46 Commando (#)	1	CU-P153	Transport	1947
Cessna UC-78 Bobcat (#)	2	?	Light transport	1947
Vultee BT-13A Valiant (#) (o)	2	?	Basic trainer	1947
Beechcraft AT-7	2	150 & 151	Multipurpose transport	1947
Beechcraft AT-11	2	160 & 161	Multipurpose transport	1947
Beechcraft F-2B	1	212	Aerial Photography	1947
Beechcraft UC-45F	1	213	Multipurpose transport	1947
Beechcraft 35 Bonanza	6	10 to 15	Air Mail	1947
Hiller H-12A	1	111	Multipurpose helicopter	1949
Lockheed C-60A Lodestar	2	214 & 215	Transport	1950
Lockheed C-56 Lodestar (=)	1	CU-EDU-1	Transport	1950
Cessna 190 (=)	1	CU-EDU-2	Light transport	1950
De Havilland Canada DHC-2 Beaver	11	15 to 19, 29 to 34	Light transport	1951-1958
Noorduyn UC-64A Norseman ($)	1	CU-CR3-C	Light transport	1951
North American NAV-4 Navion	1	?	Light transport/liaison	1951

(*) Briefly used by the CAEC and then transferred to the ANACRA civil pilot training.
(+) Not accepted by the CAEC and redelivered to Venezuela.
(#) Former FAERA aircraft.
(o) Transferred to ANACRA.
(=) Transferred to the Ministry of Education.
($) Operated by the Cuban Red Cross.

Table 7: FAN aircraft types 1928-1958[2]

Aircraft	No. of aircraft	Serials	Role	Year of acquisition
Atlantic Aircraft (Fokker) F.9 Universal	1	-	Transport with floats	1928
De Havilland DH.60GM Moth	1	N-I-1	Primary trainer/light transport	1935
Curtiss Fledgling	1	N-I-2	Primary trainer/liaison	1935
Keystone-Loening K-84 Commuter	1	3	Transport flying boat	1935
WACO Model 10/GXE	1	4	Liaison/light transport	1936
Lockheed Sirius 8A	1	10	Utility transport	1936
Stinson SR-9D Reliant	1	51	Transport	1937
WACO UMF-3	3	26 to 28 (+)	Light attack	1938
Howard DGA-8	1	58	Utility transport	1940
Howard DGA-15W	1	54	Utility transport	1940
Ford 4-AT Trimotor	3	52, 53 & 55	Transport	1941-1946
Grumman JRF-5 Goose	2	56 & 57	Transport amphibian	1942
Vought OS2U-3 Kingfisher	3	30 to 32. Later 49 to 51	ASW/Reconnaissance	1942
Naval Aircraft Factory N3N-1	3	42 to 44	Primary trainer	1943
Curtiss SO3C Seamew	3	45 to 47	Observation/Sea Patrol	1943
Consolidated PBY-5A Catalina	2	70 & 71	ASW/Maritime patrol	1950
Consolidated PBY-5A Catalina	2	72 & 73	ASW/Maritime patrol	1952
Consolidated OA-10 Catalina (#)	2	190 & 191	ASW/Maritime patrol	1954
Grumman TBM-3S2 Avenger	7	60 to 66	Torpedo bomber	1956
Sikorsky S.55 (*)	2	?	SAR/transport	1958

(+) They were later reserialled as 514 to 516. (*) Not delivered. (#) Former FAEC aircraft.

Table 8: Cuban Armed Forces ranks[3]

Army & Air Force	Navy
General Jefe (Chief General)	Almirante (Admiral)
Teniente General (Lieutenant General)	Contra Almirante (Rear Admiral)
Mayor General (Major General)	Comodoro (Commodore)
General de Brigada (Brigadier General)	Capitán de Navío (Ship Captain)
Brigadier (Brigadier)	Capitán de Fragata (Frigate Captain)
Coronel (Colonel)	Capitán de Corbeta (Corvette Captain)
Teniente Coronel (Lieutenant Colonel)	Teniente de Navío (Ship Lieutenant)
Comandante (Commandant)	Alférez de Navío (Ship Ensign)
Capitán (Captain)	Alférez de Fragata (Frigate Ensign)
Teniente Primero (First Lieutenant)	Alumnos Aspirantes (Officer Candidate)
Teniente Segundo (Second Lieutenant)	Sub Oficial (NCO)
Sub Teniente (Sub Lieutenant)	Sargento Primero (First Sergeant)
Sargento Primero (First Sergeant)	Sargento Segundo (Second Sergeant)
Sargento Segundo (Second Sergeant)	Sargento Tercero (Third Sergeant)
Sargento Tercero (Third Sergeant)	Cabo (Corporal)
Cabo (Corporal)	Marinero de Primera (First Class Sailor)
Soldado (Soldier)	Marinero de Segunda (Second Calss Sailor)
Conscripto Servicio Militar (Military Service Conscript)	Conscripto Servicio Militar (Military Service Conscript)

ENDNOTES

Chapter 2

1. The Cuban Eight manoeuvre was invented by Len Povey and consists of 5/8ths of a loop to the 45-degree line, a 1/2 roll, 6/8ths of a loop to the 45-degree line, a 1/2 roll, and 1/8th of a loop to level flight.

Chapter 3

1. Daniel P. Hagedorn, *Central American and Caribbean Air Forces* (Tonbridge, UK: Air-Britain (Historians), 1993).

Chapter 4

1. Marilú Uralde Cancio and Luis Rosado *Eiró, El ejército soy yo. Las fuerzas armadas de Cuba (1952-1956)* (La Habana: Editorial de Ciencias Sociales, 2006).

Chapter 5

1. Daniel P. Hagedorn and Mario Overall, *The Caribbean Legion and Its Mercenary Air Forces 1947-1950* (Yolanda, UK: Lime Tree Press, 2021).

Chapter 6

1. Hagedorn, *Central American Air Forces.*

Chapter 7

1. Hagedorn, *Central American Air Forces.*
2. Dan Hagedorn, 'Latin Mitchells: North American B-25s in South America, Part Four', *Air Enthusiast Magazine*, 108 (December 2003).

Appendix

1. Hagedorn, *Central American Air Forces.*
2. Hagedorn, *Central American Air Forces.*
3. Hagedorn, *Central American Air Forces.*

SOURCES

Books

Ameringer, Charles D., *The Caribbean Legion: Patriots, Politicians, Soldiers of Fortune, 1946-1950* (University Park, PA: Pennsylvania State University Press, 1996)

Andrade, John M., *Latin-American Military Aviation.* First Edition. (Leicester, UK: Midland Counties Publications, 1982)

Argote-Freyre, Frank, *Fulgencio Batista: From Revolutionary to Strongman.* Vol. 1. (New Brunswick, NJ: Rutgers University Press, 2006)

Batista, Fulgencio, *Cuba Betrayed* (New York: Vantage Press, 1962)

Batista, Fulgencio, *The Growth and Decline of the Cuban Republic* (New York: The Devin-Adair Company, 1964)

Butler, Phil, and Dan Hagedorn, *Air Arsenal North America: Aircraft for the Allies 1938-1945, Purchases and Lend-Lease* (Hinkley, UK: Midland Publishing, 2004)

Carreras Rivery, Raquel, *Alas Cubanas sobre el Continente Americano: Oscar Rivery y el Vuelo de la Solidaridad de la Aviación Naval de Cuba 1940-1941* (Columbia, SC: Edi ADIHNC, 2020)

Chivalette, William I., and W. Parker-Hayes Jr, *Balloons on High: The History of Early Enlisted Aeronautics, 1862 to 1907* (Suitland, MD: Airmen Memorial Museum, 1986)

Dean, Francis H., and Dan Hagedorn, *Curtiss Fighter Aircraft: A Photographic History 1917-1948* (Atglen, PA: Schiffer Military History, 2007)

De León, Calixto Albertos, *Esto es un Ocho Cubano! Los Curtiss Hawk export model* (Santa Cruz de Tenerife, Spain: Grafiexpress S.L., 2019)

Duque de Estrada, Rolando Marrón, *Los precursores de la aviación en Cuba* (Barcelona: Editorial de Ciencias Sociales, 2021)

Espinosa Casas, Edelberto, *Cuba desde el aire. Memoria y anécdotas de un aviador* (Miami, FL: Letras Latinas Publishing, 2021)

Fermoselle, Rafael, *The Evolution of the Cuban Military, 1492-1986* (Miami, FL: Ediciones Universal, 1987)

Hagedorn, Daniel P., *Central American and Caribbean Air Forces* (Tonbridge, UK: Air-Britain (Historians), 1993)

Hagedorn, Dan, and Mario Overall, *The Caribbean Legion and Its Mercenary Air Forces 1947-1950* (Yolanda, UK: Lime Tree Press, 2021)

Hagedorn, Dan, *Latin American Air Wars and aircraft 1912-1969* (Crowborough, UK: Hikoki Publications, 2005)

Hagedorn, Dan, *P-38 in Latin America.* 1st Edition (Aviation Art & HistoRy, 2022)

Hagedorn, Dan, *Republic P-47 Thunderbolt: The Final Chapter, Latin American Air Forces Service* (St. Paul, MN: Phalanx Publishing, 1991)

Hagedorn, Dan, *Texans and Harvards in Latin America* (Staplefield, UK: Air Britain (Historians), 2009)

Higuchi, Hélio, and Paulo Roberto Bastos Junior, *Cuban Migs: The Defenders of Castro's Force* (Vienna: Harpia Publishing, 2022)

Legg, David, *Consolidated PBY Catalina: The Peacetime Record* (Shrewsbury, UK: Airlife Publishing, 2002)

Mallin Sr, Jay, *History of the Cuban Armed Forces: From Colony to Castro* (Reston, VA: Ancient Mariners Press, 2000)

Nijenhuis, Wim, *Mitchell Masterpieces.* Vol. 2, *An Illustrated History of Paint Jobs on B-25s in Foreign Military Service* (Odoorn: Lanasta, 2009)

Overall, Mario, and Dan Hagedorn, *Douglas DC-3/C-47 in Latin American Military Service* (Manchester, UK: Crécy Publishing, 2021)

Puersan, Luis P., *La historia de la aviación militar Dominicana. Desde sus inicios a su decadencia* (Orlando, FL: Author's edition, 2022)

Rivas, Santiago, *British Combat Aircraft in Latin America* (Manchester, UK: Crécy Publishing, 2019)

Somers, Robert, *The Cuban Eight* (Greer, SC: PAS/Professional Aviation Services, 2010)

Uralde Cancio, Marilú and Luis Rosado Eiró, *El ejército soy yo. Las fuerzas armadas de Cuba (1952-1956)* (La Habana: Editorial de Ciencias Sociales, 2006)

Whitney, Robert W, *State and Revolution in Cuba: Mass Mobilization and Political Change, 1920–1940* (Chapel Hill, NC: The University of North Carolina Press, 2001)

Articles

Hagedorn, Dan, and Mario Overall, 'The Making of a Mercenary Air Force', *LAAHS*, <https://www.laahs.com/mercenary-air-force/>, accessed 16 July 2025

Hagedorn, Dan, 'Latin Mitchells: North American B-25s in South America, Part Four', *Air Enthusiast Magazine*, 108 (December 2003)

Conferences

Ibarra Guitart, Dr. Jorge Renato, *La Expedición de Cayo Confites. Su Escenario Hemisférico*. Instituto de Historia de Cuba. Lecture given at the XVIII Congress organised by Asociación Mexicana de Estudios del Caribe A.C in Querétaro, Mexico on 25 to 27 April 2012

Web pages

Cuban Aviation on several Facebook pages:

Nuestra Fuerza Aérea. Su Historia
Veteranos de la Aviación Cubana
Historia de la Aviación Militar Cubana (H.A.M.C.)
Anécdotas y Relatos de la Aviación

Cuban Naval Aviation at *https://www.facebook.com/aidhnc555* (*Asociación para la Investigación y Difusión de la Historia Naval de Cuba*)

Cuban Military Aviation at *http://www.urrib2000.narod.ru*

Cuban Military Aviation history at *http://avstop.com/history/aroundtheworld/cuba/cuba.html*

ABOUT THE AUTHORS

Hélio Higuchi was born in São Paulo, Brazil on 12 November 1953. He graduated in Architecture and Urban Planning, with a postgraduate degree in Marketing, and has been working in the hotel sector. His main hobby is doing research on military history and its respective equipment in Latin American countries. He is the author of several books on Latin American military aviation and armoured vehicles, as well as numerous articles in specialised magazines based in Brazil, the United States and the UK.

Antonio Luis Sapienza Fracchia was born in Asunción, Paraguay on 14 May 1960. He graduated from the Catholic University of Asunción where he graduated with a B.A. in Clinical Psychology. He has also taken specialised English courses at Tulane University in New Orleans, Louisiana, and in teaching methodology at San Diego State University in California. He is now retired but worked for nearly 40 years as an English Teacher and as one of the Academic Coordinators at the Centro Cultural Paraguayo-Americano (CCPA), a binational institute in Asunción. Married with two children, he resides in the capital. He is an aviation historian who has written more than 500 articles in specialised magazines and web pages on Paraguayan aviation history and has given numerous lectures in schools, universities, institutes, military and civil institutions in Paraguay and abroad. Since 2004, he has been an aviation history professor with the Paraguayan Air Force (FAP). In August 2023, he was appointed corresponding academician at the Paraguayan Academy of History. He has published twenty-eight books since 1996, the present volume being his fifteenth with Helion. He has received a total of seven decorations for his academic merits, two from Argentina, one from Brazil and four from his own country, Paraguay, including two from the air force, one from naval viation and one from the Civil Aviation Authority DINAC.